WINNING THE
GAME OF WORK

# WINNING THE GAME OF WORK

## CAREER HAPPINESS AND SUCCESS ON YOUR OWN TERMS

By Terry Boyle
McDougall

NEW DEGREE PRESS

COPYRIGHT © 2020 TERRY BOYLE MCDOUGALL

WINNING THE GAME OF WORK

*Career Happiness and Success on Your Own Terms*

| ISBN | 978-1-64137-580-1 | *Paperback* |
| | 978-1-64137-581-8 | *Kindle Ebook* |
| | 978-1-64137-582-5 | *Ebook* |

*This book is dedicated to all the smart, hardworking people*
*who want more from work than just a paycheck.*

# CONTENTS

———

*Imagine what a harmonious world it could be if every single person, both young and old, shared a little of what he is good at doing.*

—QUINCY JONES

# ACKNOWLEDGMENTS

———

When I left my corporate job in 2017, I began blogging as a way to process my transition to entrepreneurship. As I posted my thoughts and observations about the meaning and dynamics of work, readers shared that the topics resonated with them. After two years of writing, I recognized those blog posts as seeds that could grow into a book if nurtured appropriately. Indeed, after more than seven months of focus, those blogs have matured into this book which I hope will be a helpful guide to people who want to be successful *and* fulfilled at work.

Writing a book is a lot like raising a child—it truly takes a village, and I want to acknowledge the village that helped me mold my thoughts and ideas into a book that anyone would consider reading.

My deepest love and appreciation always to my husband Scott, who has been my biggest fan and supporter for almost thirty years. Without you, I wouldn't have gotten half as far in life or had a quarter of the fun. Thanks to my awesome kids, Brady, Cam, and Caroline. I'm so proud to be your mom! To Gabby, who was at my side as I wrote nearly every word in this book—you are the best dog in the world.

This book would also not have been possible without those who helped me heal, grow, and gain perspective on my own life and career. I'm thankful for the Hoffman Institute, iPEC, The Second City Training Center, and the wonderful people I met through those programs for helping me see more clearly how much power we each have to determine our own paths in life. The freedom and empowerment you helped me discover is priceless.

Sincere thanks to the mentors and coaches along the way who had faith in me and helped me understand the unwritten rules of the game of work: Dennis Moriarty, Ed Hutchins, Janice Westmoreland, Mack Myer, Maura Koutoujian, Pamela Corbin, Raj Madan, Rick Kuwayti, Stephanie Meis, Steve Fleshman and many more.

I was given Richard N. Bolles's book *What Color is Your Parachute?* as a college graduation gift back in 1986. I credit that book with shifting my mindset at the start of my career to realize that it just makes sense to align one's strengths and preferences with what you do for a living. Though Richard passed away in 2017, I am honored and thankful that his son, Gary A. Bolles, who is himself an expert on career planning and the future of work, lent me his time and insights for the book.

I am also deeply grateful to the individuals who allowed me to share their career stories: Andrew Linderman, Colette

Aaron[1], Holly Segur, Jennifer C. Dowling, Judge Deborah Day[1], Laura Yunger, Matt Ryder[1], Paul Rudolph[1], and Scott Wentworth. Thank you for openly relating both the triumphs and difficulties you experienced as you sought to lead authentic and meaningful careers. Your stories provide a depth and humanity that enrich the book. I want to also acknowledge the people who provided valuable perspective that helped mold the book: Colleen McFarland, Herman Jaramillo, and Jonathan Palk.

Thanks to all the wise and patient people at the B-School program and New Degree Press. I appreciate the guidance and encouragement you provided and for showing me that writing a book can be a relatively pain-free process: Eric Koester, Brian Bies, Cortni Merritt, Christi Martin, Kristy Carter, Amanda Brown, my fellow program authors and everyone behind the scenes at these organizations.

Thanks to all of the friends and supporters who pre-ordered the book, read and commented on chapters, and provided encouragement during the process. Without you, this book would not look like it does today. I feel so blessed to have walked the same path with you, even if for just a little while: Adam Cody, Aimee Renkes, Alison Keefe, Andrew Schumacher, Anita Wilson, Ann Shufflebarger, Barbara Belligio, Betsey Leggat, Bradley Robert Trick, Brady McDougall, Charles Thornton, Cheryl Wittenstein, Christina Lis, Christine O'Neill, Claire Kalb, Dahlia Hanin, Darby Sorber, Deb from BC, Deb Wall, Denise Bays, Dominic Perri, Emilie

---

[1] The names of some interview subjects were changed at their request to preserve their privacy.

Totten, Eric Koester, Erin Terpack, Eric Zoberman, Eva Reid, Felicia Hudson, Galit Ben Ari, Jane Evans, Janine MacLachlan, Jen Ostrich, Jennifer Alberts, Jennifer Dowling, Jennifer Santucci, Joe Rosenthal, Joel Bennett, Joel Landis, Julie Breckenfelder, Julie Little, Karen Butler, Karen Johnson, Karen Murray, Kate Covey, Kate Liebelt, Keith Lawrance, Kelly Kalb, Ken Silber, Kevin Hanson, Kristin Warren, Laura Davies, Laura Honeycutt, Laura Yunger, Laurie Anderson, Laurie Greenburg, Laurie Lynch, Marianne Hewitt, Marisa Williams, Marsha Hope, Matt Cornelison, Matt Gruchala, Matt Perry, Maulik Bhagat, Michael S. Greenbaum, Michael Wapner, Mike Bass, Nicole Frier, Pamela Spadino, Pam Schwartz, Patti Ernst, Paul Adornato, Paul Barnett, Paul Bobnak, Paul Mason, Paul Sutenbach, Paul Thomas Hickman, Paula Johnson, Peg Dowgwilla, Pete Montalvo, Pete Owsiak, Rachel Winer, Rana Lee, Rick Bolnick, Robbin Sejud, Robert Waggoner, Ronald Axe, Rose McInerney, Stephanie Meis, Stephen Williams, Suzanne Hart, Tami Chapek, Tammy Gianfortune, Tim Fohner, Tim Hartnett, Wanda Whitson, Ward Bumby, Weiyan Zhao, Wendy Mages, William McDougall III, and William McDougall, Jr.

I wrote this book because I believe each of us is here for a reason, and the sooner we embrace our purpose in life and at work and show up as ourselves, the happier we will be and the better the world will be. Thank you for helping me step more fully into my own reason for being.

# HOW TO "PLAY" THIS BOOK

———

I believe that the more you listen to yourself and follow your own instincts, the happier you'll be. So, in that spirit, I encourage you to read this book in the way that works best for you. You make up the rules. Here are some suggestions for how to "play" the book:

### IDENTIFY WHAT YOU WANT FROM THE BOOK

Did you pick up this book because you were curious and wanted to learn more? Or do you have a clear objective that you'd like to achieve by a specific deadline?

Any objective you have is completely legitimate. You can decide how to use this book depending on your endgame. You can make it into a treasure hunt. Here's how: write out five questions that you hope the book will answer for you, then go look for the answers.

## SKIM IT OR READ IT STRAIGHT THROUGH

You don't need to finish the book to get value from it, so go ahead and start reading. If something grabs your attention, take notes and act. See if you notice any differences once you start viewing work as a game and becoming a more accomplished player.

## USE THE STRUCTURE AS A GUIDE

The book is made up of four sections:

1. What's Your Objective?
2. Learning the Rules of the Game
3. Taking Your Game to the Next Level
4. Becoming a Champion

## BE INSPIRED

In my coaching practice, clients often ask the question,

> *"Do other people have the same*
> *fears or challenges that I do?"*

The answer is, "Of course!"

In the book, you'll find stories from fascinating people[2] who share the good, bad, and ugly of their career journeys. Their

---

2   The career stories included in the book are based on interviews with individuals and have been edited and condensed for clarity. In the cases where real names have been used, it is with their permission. Otherwise, names and identifying details have been changed to protect the privacy of the individuals at their request. In some cases, stories rely on characters to illustrate common patterns of behavior I've observed in the workplace and are not based on any specific individual.

experiences illustrate many of the book's key tenets. I hope you find their stories inspirational as you walk with them through both their struggles and triumphs.

## SKIP LIBERALLY

Skip anything that doesn't grab your attention. Each chapter stands on its own, so feel free to flip to the next chapter or read one of the career stories if a certain chapter isn't grabbing you.

## TAKE ACTION

Nothing will happen unless you take action. Questions and exercises are sprinkled throughout the book. As you read, I encourage you to keep a journal or notebook nearby to jot down notes and answer the exercise questions in chapters throughout.

As you gain new insights, you'll be amazed by how fun the game of work can be once you see the whole game board and implement new, more effective strategies, winning on your own terms.

## CELEBRATE YOUR VICTORIES

High achievers are notorious for being so focused on their goals that they don't take the time to savor their wins. As you experience positive outcomes in your career, take the time to celebrate and enjoy your accomplishments. You deserve it!

# INTRODUCTION

———

*It would be so much easier if I could just be a student instead of always a pawn in a bigger game.*

—SARAH K. L. WILSON[3]

I was blindsided.

Okay, maybe I should have seen this coming, but I was just a babe in the woods at the time. Barely a year out of college, working my first job at a magazine publisher in Boston.

My boss, Dennis, got a new boss. It didn't really impact him at first. Dennis continued to do what he'd always done—sell magazine advertising. When he had the chance to sell one more ad for the issue that had just closed, he did what had always worked in the past.

---

3    Wilson, Sarah K. L. *Dragon School:* Sworn. N.p.: INDEPENDENTLY PUBLISHED, 2018.

He threw his weight around with the head of production to get the ad into that issue. The only problem was that Dennis's new boss, Pete, wasn't budging on the new policy he'd put in place. Pete's view was that once the book closed, it stayed closed.

What happened next is a matter of disagreement.

Dennis says he was fired.

Pete says he quit.

All I knew was that my happy little work family was suddenly missing one gregarious leader. As Dennis was escorted from the building, little did I know at the time, along with him went my promised promotion.

My earnest desire was to move up in the world of 1980s publishing . . . but a few weeks later, the dust of Dennis's departure had settled and Mike, the new sales manager, had been hired; it was a whole new ball game.

Though I'd paid my dues as a bright and valued supporter of the sales team and been seen by Dennis as a rising associate ready to move to the next level, Mike saw me only as an administrative assistant with no tangible experience in marketing.

He interviewed me for the marketing coordinator role, but it soon became clear that he'd only been going through the motions. He hired an external candidate with an associate degree and one year working as a marketing coordinator for a local hotel.

In Mike's estimation, my eighteen months of service at the firm and BA in Economics didn't equate to the value his new marketing hire brought. I was incensed. To him I was nothing special—just someone who was already there when he started. Kind of like the office furniture. Even today I am still stunned, but no longer surprised, at how unfair his decision was. With many years of hindsight, I see a lot of things now that were invisible to me at the time.

Now I know I just hadn't yet been initiated into how the game of work is played. It was the first of many lessons that would follow.

## WHY I WROTE THIS BOOK

Over the course of my career, it dawned on me that the rules I learned in school weren't the same rules that governed the business world. Every time I expected things to be "fair" based on my read of the situations, I was disappointed.

It eventually occurred to me that something deeper was going on, and I was determined to figure out what it was. I hope you'll find some insights to help make your path to your own career success and satisfaction a little smoother.

## THERE'S MORE TO WORK THAN YOU REALIZE

This book is for anyone who has experienced confusion about the mysterious things that happen at work—those days when you think you're following the rules, but you don't get the outcome you expect.

I bet you would prefer a career where you enjoy success and happiness rather than a grinding job that causes you nothing but stress and misery. You were drawn to the professional world because you like to solve complex problems and be rewarded for it. My guess is that you are smart and talented—after all, you picked up this book!

You probably figured, "Hey, this is America—the land of opportunity. I'm smart, hardworking, and ambitious. What else do I need to succeed?" Indeed, that's the attitude I had more than thirty years ago when I first started my career. I'd been successful in school. What could be different in the workplace? It didn't take long to realize I had a lot to learn.

## THIS IS NOT TURNING OUT HOW I EXPECTED

I've learned many lessons the hard way. When I look back to the start of my career, it's now easy to see how clueless I was. I was an earnest "good girl" who believed that if I studied the "rules" and followed them, was polite and cooperative, kept my head down and my nose clean, and didn't complain, I'd get what was coming to me: advancement, raises, titles, growth opportunities—the works. I mean, that approach had worked for me throughout seventeen years of school and even for the first year or so after college.

But it was as if the business world said to me, "What a naive little thing you are. Keep bringing your best, and we'll keep using you. And don't think you'll get any particular recognition for just doing your job."

## WHERE YOU'RE COMING FROM

Maybe you're a recent college graduate, and you're learning the ropes in your first job. Or perhaps you're a corporate veteran who has worked for many companies and has given up trying to make sense of the weird things that go on in your workplace. You may be committed to your company and want to be effective in your current role, or maybe you're actively looking for a new job.

Regardless of where you are in your career, I'm certain of one thing: you'd like to be happy with the bargain of trading your time and talents for money, benefits, and if you're lucky, fulfillment. You want to know that your work matters. You want to be seen and validated. You want to learn and grow.

It's sometimes hard to understand what you can do to make that happen. Even when you follow the written rules, you may notice that things don't always turn out as expected. You run into unforeseen obstacles. People who seem less talented than you move ahead, and you're not sure why. It can be downright puzzling, even infuriating.

## HOW CAN WORK BE A GAME?

If you're working hard, following the rules and not experiencing the outcomes you desire, it's because of one thing: you are playing the game of work by the wrong rules! You may think, "Game of work? What is she smoking? Work is not a game. It's serious business! My livelihood depends on this."

Fair enough. Work *is* serious. But understanding how to navigate at work will help you achieve your professional goals.

That's precisely why I look at work as a game. Games, like work, have objectives, rules, and strategies you use when playing them.

## MONOPOLY BY THE RULES OF TWISTER

When people are confused by the results they are achieving at work, it's usually because they don't understand the objectives, are playing by the wrong rules, or have no strategy—one that takes the wrong factors into consideration.

So it's no wonder they are frustrated. It's like trying to win Monopoly when you're playing with the rules from Twister.

## LEARNING TO PLAY THE GAME OF WORK

This book is about shifting your perspective and learning some of the unwritten rules that no one tells you. I'll share new ways of looking at the things that go on at work so you can clearly see the whole "game board" and develop strategies for how to maneuver to win. This new set of rules will enable you to more effectively navigate your career in business.

The unwritten rules often seem counterintuitive. It took me years to make sense of this—to see that a whole other reality was beneath what I could see. I'd observed others who didn't follow what seemed to be the most basic rules—they'd be late for meetings, turn in reports late, and be uncommunicative—yet they moved ahead. I was perplexed. It seemed unfair. What was going on? The bottom line was that they knew the real rules and what to focus on, and I didn't.

## WHAT'S IN STORE FOR YOU

In this book, I'll tell my own stories and some from fascinating people who shared their hard-won career lessons with me. The thing to remember is that no one's success is ever preordained. Though we see people who are currently successful, it's important to acknowledge that along the way, they made mistakes and had moments of uncertainty and even failure.

They didn't know which choices would result in the outcomes they got. It's only in looking back on their careers that we see those pivotal moments that led them to their present success. In examining those moments, you can learn lessons to apply to your own journey.

## TENACIOUSLY SEEKING THE *WHY*

I've always been drawn to complex challenges. When I was a kid, my mother compared me to a tenacious little terrier. Once I got hold of something, I wouldn't let it go until I figured it out. Indeed, even today, my mind always runs through scenarios, observing and trying to understand the flow of information, the motivations of people, and how systems work. I always want to know why things happen. Frankly, it drives me crazy when I can't puzzle something out.

To better understand how to be successful in the corporate world, I read scores of business and leadership books, countless articles, and white papers published by top business schools and consulting firms. I've gone to many training courses, absorbed the wisdom of experienced mentors, and worked with executive coaches to help me navigate and influence.

My interest in understanding systems and the factors that contribute to how they work is what drew me to economics as my major in college. The economy is driven by many factors—interest rates, consumer confidence, weather, the stock market, international trade, and even presidential tweets. It's a mix of many components, influences, and forces.

## USING THE INFLUENCE THAT YOU HAVE

We all take part in this system, and no one really controls it. Though it may not feel like it, what each of us do impacts the economy in a small way. The same is true in the workplace. Whether you're in the lowest entry-level position or you're the CEO, what you do impacts the organization's success. The trick is to recognize that and see the ripple effect you create, then learn how to control it.

If you're not the CEO, I understand if you're a little skeptical about how a book can help you make a bigger impact. However, keep an open mind. Recognize that maybe work is more than the rules you've believed until now and be willing to try some new things.

As you absorb the lessons in this book, I feel confident you'll understand work in a new way. You'll see the unwritten rules beneath the rules you've been taught. When you understand the extent of your own power, what motivates people around you, what you really want, and how you add value, you'll see work in a whole new way.

## THE PURPOSE OF THIS BOOK

I learned lessons during my career that helped me see the underlying dynamics of what happens at work and why. Once I could see the dynamics, I could understand how to influence the corporate ecosystems in which I worked. The purpose of this book is to shed light on these unwritten rules so you can maneuver and get the opportunities, rewards, and recognition you deserve.

Just a note about some of the language in the book: I worked for corporations for the majority of my career, but the lessons of this book can also be applied in other work environments such as education, government, and nonprofits.

## SEEING THE WHOLE GAME BOARD

My goal is to shift your perspective on what happens at work so you can see the whole game board and understand what moves you have available. We usually have more options than we believe. Seeing hose additional options will give you courage to try different approaches to achieve the results you want out of your career. It can be natural to feel fear when trying unfamiliar approaches when deviating from what has worked in the past.

When faced with a leap of faith to try something different, I ask you, do you want to continue to ignore the unwritten rules and get the same outcome you've gotten in the past? Once again bypassed for a raise or promotion? Once again not getting the sorely needed extra resources? Or would you rather live by the unwritten rules and see your efforts pay off as you achieve the levels of success and rewards you're capable of?

## GET OFF THE SIDELINES AND INTO THE GAME

Many clients tell me that office politics is an area they find distasteful, inscrutable, and uncomfortable, and they want to avoid it. I can understand that; politics can feel unseemly. People who are good at it sometimes seem more influential without providing much value.

True, some players can use smoke and mirrors—and take credit for other people's work—to move up the corporate ladder. But take a moment and focus on the key word here: *influence*. When you focus on the value you bring to your organization *and* learn how to play the game of work, you'll have more influence and probably be more satisfied with your efforts.

The purpose of this book is to shed light on these unwritten rules so you can maneuver and get the opportunities, rewards, and recognition you deserve.

## BEEN THERE, DONE THAT

Though my dream to be a marketing leader came true after decades, I found myself less enthused about my career. I didn't feel the same sense of satisfaction and accomplishment that I'd enjoyed earlier. I had been there, done that, and bought the t-shirt. After much deliberation, in 2017, I left my job to find a livelihood that suited me better. The tough part was figuring out what it would be.

Before leaving my last job, I was given a farewell party. I was touched when several people thanked me for coaching and mentoring them. Some said they believed they wouldn't have advanced as quickly in their careers without my encouragement and support.

Though I loved managing people, I wasn't aware that the investment of my time and effort had a positive impact. It was gratifying to realize that others had received value from something I loved doing! Those conversations stuck with me.

## STARTING A NEW CAREER

After leaving my job, I briefly hung up a shingle as a marketing consultant. I loved the newfound freedom, but it just felt like more of what I'd already done. Then, through networking, I was introduced to Lara Siegel, who left a successful career in public relations to become a career coach. It was evident she loved her new profession.

She told me about the coach training program she had gone through. I was intrigued and looked into it. Within weeks, I was enrolled and began training to become a certified professional coach. Twice during my career, I had hired coaches to help me develop skills and gain clarity around challenges I faced at work—and now I was on my way to a new career helping others do the same thing.

## A NATURAL ALIGNMENT

This new path seemed like a great fit. Throughout my life, I enjoyed helping friends and coworkers feel more confident, reach their goals, and be more satisfied with themselves, their lives, and their careers. I liked being the cheerleader who helped people see they were more capable, wonderful, intelligent, and, yes, lovable than they gave themselves credit for.

As a manager, I'd often be in an update meeting with a team member and look across the table at this incredibly talented person sharing their doubts about some aspect of their job. I was motivated to support them as they aligned their confidence with their true potential. I realized I'd always been a coach—even back in elementary school when I'd help kids with their math—and now, I'm formally trained and certified. It feels amazing to be on a path that is innate to who I am.

## AM I CRAZY?

I want to share what I've learned as I've been on this journey. Sometimes I think I was crazy to consciously walk away from a job when I was the primary breadwinner for my family of five.

Working as a leader in a big company is great in so many ways . . . we got to do big things. I loved being part of a team focused on making our company successful. I can think of nothing better than completing a project that almost seemed impossible at the start. It was satisfying when the business met its goals, and the bonuses were nice, too!

## THE PROS AND CONS OF "BIG"

Large organizations offer countless opportunities for learning new skills, taking on challenges, and advancing internally, which is exciting and rewarding. I also know the obstacles that exist in large and complex organizations—inscrutable political dynamics, scant exposure to decision makers in far-off head offices, and mismatched expectations that make it difficult to demonstrate your talents—to name a few. With this book, I hope to help you navigate the often-murky waters of managing your career and help you sail into a place of professional success and personal satisfaction.

# PART 1

# WHAT'S YOUR OBJECTIVE?

## CHAPTER 1

# WORK IS A GAME

———

*Nothing is like it seems, but*
*everything is exactly like it is.*

—YOGI BERRA[4]

## HOW CAN WORK BE A GAME?

After more than thirty years working and coaching hundreds of professionals on success, I know work is essentially a game.

Work encompasses the activities you do to earn money to buy the stuff you and your loved ones need for survival—as well as enjoyment. You may have worked hard to gain the education and experience required to do your job. In addition, part of your identity may be tied to what you do for a living.

———

4 "Yogi Berra Quote." Quotefancy.com. Accessed February 1, 2020.

Think about how often "What do you do?" and "Who do you work for?" come up in casual conversations with acquaintances. For better or worse, people rank and categorize our place in society based on our work.

In contrast, games are activities we usually take part in for fun. If you lose a game, you might say, "No big deal. I'll get 'em next time." However, if you lose your job, that probably won't be your reaction. So, I get it. It feels weird to frame work as a game, because work is such an important organizing force in your life. But that's precisely why I propose that you look at it this way. It provides much-needed perspective.

## GAINING OBJECTIVITY TO BE STRATEGIC

We can get so attached to our work that we have a hard time being objective about it. It's so personal. I see it all the time in my coaching practice when clients experience difficulty at work. It's natural to get emotionally involved in what's going on and feel helpless, hopeless, or angry and at a loss about how to make the situation better. This causes stress, which spills over and affects personal relationships and health— physically and mentally.

If you think about it, work and games have many things in common. Much like a game, work has an objective, which in for-profit businesses, is making money, and it has rules about how you play, as well as strategies that employees use to get ahead. The advantage of viewing work as a game is that it creates some distance between you as the "player" and the dynamics of the business.

It enables you to see the larger game board and opportunities that would be impossible to see when you're in the middle of the activity. When you understand this, you can be more strategic and focus on achieving longer-term goals.

When you fail to create this type of distance, you can't see the whole board, and this can leave you feeling like a pawn. If you can't see what's going on around you, you can't be strategic. When you leave yourself no moves, you are at the mercy of savvy players. That can leave you feeling helpless, and no one wants to feel that way.

## THERE'S MORE TO WORK THAN IT SEEMS

I used to look at the workplace dynamic as a simplistic relationship between employer and employee. The business had an objective—to make money. The employer made up the rules of how that would happen, decided what the employees would do—or not do—to deliver the value that customers paid for.

The employees showed up, performed the activities associated with their roles, picked up a paycheck, and went home. Wash, rinse, repeat. The employees who did their jobs in a superlative way would naturally be recognized and promoted. It seemed simple.

Maybe you picked up this book because, in your career, it's become apparent that it's not that simple after all. You might feel a little lost, even cheated, if you're not getting the results you expect from your efforts at work.

Your frustration is understandable. If you're confused about where you are and about the rules of unsuccess that you have to unlearn, your feelings are justified. Let's work through it. The best revenge is success, right? So let the lessons begin.

## PLAYING BY THE WRONG RULES

If you're not getting success and satisfaction from your job, it may be because work really is a game, and you don't know the rules. After all, if you're not achieving the objectives you desire, then something is not working.

Many factors can contribute to unattained goals. However, if you're experienced, working hard on the right things, and still not getting the results you desire, you could be metaphorically playing Monopoly by Twister's rules.

## IT'S DÉJÀ VU ALL OVER AGAIN

I started this chapter with a quote widely attributed to Yogi Berra. He was a catcher with the New York Yankees for eighteen seasons from the 1940s to the 1960s, and though he holds the record for the most World Series Championships as a player—ten [5]—he is arguably best known nowadays for his quirky quotes. Even if you're not familiar with Berra, you've probably heard, or even repeated, some of his sayings, such as, "It ain't over till it's over," "It's déjà vu all over again," and "When you come to a fork in the road, take it."[6]

---

5    Posnanski, Joe. "The Meaning of Yogi: It's déjà vu all over again." Sports Illustrated, July 4, 2011, pp. 64–66.

6    Berra, Yogi. The Yogi Book. Workman Publishing, 1998, p. 9.

The fascinating thing about these "Yogisms," and a large part of why his name is still brought up today, is the ironic wisdom they contain. At face value, the sayings contradict themselves and make no sense, yet a deeper truth comes from them that isn't perceived initially. Like the quote at the beginning of this chapter, there can be a big difference between what seems to be and what actually is.

## START PLAYING BY THE "RIGHT" RULES

When you're in the middle of your work and unable to recognize that you're on a playing field, you may think you know what's going on. You know the "rules" and are following them to the T. You're working hard and expecting to earn the rewards, but then someone else gets the recognition or raise or promotion, and you're left wondering what the heck went wrong. You may feel robbed or cheated. You may want to blame those who received the reward you were expecting. After all, *you* are the one playing by the rules, and they aren't.

The reality is that they are playing Monopoly by the rules of Monopoly, and you're playing by some other rules that you believe are the proper rules, but they may actually be the rules to Twister. Because you don't understand the game, you're twisting yourself into a pretzel trying to win Twister while your colleague is calmly putting hotels on Boardwalk and collecting all the rewards that go with it.

That's where the wisdom of Berra's saying comes in . . . Nothing is like it seems. Yet it is what it is. You can continue to operate based on what you think the rules are or what you think they should be, or you can take a step back, see the dynamic of what's really going on at your work, and base your actions on what *is*.

## ON THE TOPIC OF CORPORATE "PLAYAHS"

Another reason why some people have a hard time viewing work as a game is thanks to the "playahs" who exist in many workplaces. People who don't seem to work as hard yet reap the rewards. Some people rise within organizations by manipulating those around them.

But others rise quickly for another reason that the rest of us should sit up and take note of: they simply understand the rules of the game of work. They show up equipped. They show up pretrained. They show up ready to play, rather than struggling to understand. Sometimes they may work shorter hours, but there's nothing wrong with that. They work for impact.

Isn't a baseball game that's won 1–0 as much of a win as a game that's 10–9? I might even argue that a game that's 1–0 is more efficient and used fewer resources.

## INSIDE BASEBALL

Many analogies in the sports world illustrate the differences between those who seem to rise effortlessly and those who toil away with little to show for it. When I was ten or eleven years old, I would play baseball with the kids in my neighborhood in an empty lot behind my house. We had no strategy. The team with the most runs when we were called home for dinner was the winning team.

Because I played sandlot baseball countless times, I thought I understood baseball. As I got older and began watching major league games, I noticed all the moves and substitutions that the managers made, and it dawned on me that baseball was a *much* deeper and more complex game than I'd understood as a child.

## TRADING TIME FOR MONEY—EASY-PEASY

Do you remember your first job? I do. I scooped ice cream at a neighborhood store for two dollars per hour. I traded my time for money. As long as I showed up for work on time, I got my paycheck every other Friday. Besides the minor drama that arises when a bunch of high school girls worked together, it was pretty simple. Show up, work, get paid. Easy-peasy.

Much the way I thought I knew the game of baseball because I played as a child, early in my post-college career, I thought I understood what it took to be successful at work because I held a few jobs between age fourteen and twenty-two.

Back then, I thought the key to success was as simple as working hard, showing my dedication, and letting my natural talent and intelligence wow my boss. I assumed I knew what to expect at my first real-world job at the publishing company. My boss liked me, I worked hard, and I figured I'd be rewarded with a promotion in no time.

## DENNIS WALKS OUT WITH MY PROMOTION

As I shared in the introduction, I had a rude awakening at my first job when I realized that ambition and hard work weren't enough to move ahead. I was so excited about the promotion that Dennis had promised me. It would be my first step out of administrative support. I would graduate from answering phones and typing letters to helping create the company's marketing strategy.

When Dennis quit—or was fired—I was still optimistic that the hard work I'd put in would be recognized and rewarded by his successor. I saw myself as bright and dedicated and felt sure that was evident to everyone around me, including Dennis's replacement, Mike. I realize now that Mike probably saw me as Dennis's girl. He had no loyalty to me and was not under any obligation to follow through on Dennis's promise to promote me.

I felt so cheated when Mike hired someone from outside to fill that role. At the time, I was naive and didn't understand anything about office politics. I didn't know that new leaders usually have their own ideas and don't typically follow the playbook left behind by their predecessor—especially when the person they replaced was fired.

To say the least, that was an eye-opener, but a valuable lesson that has served me well in my career since then. It trained me to step back and look at the larger playing field—not just at the moves that I thought the other players were going to make. When circumstances change, everything else can change as well.

## IT TAKES MORE THAN TALENT

You may believe that if you get educated, get a good job with a great company, and work hard, you'll ascend the ranks of your organization, be recognized as a leader, and make lots of money. But, as many smart, overachieving professionals have discovered, that's not all there is to getting ahead at work.

It's like a naturally gifted athlete thinking that, if he got drafted by the New York Yankees, with some grit and hard work, he'd soon be wearing a World Series ring. The reality is that talent is only one factor required to achieve that goal.

Advancing at work also depends on:

- What you do to improve your skills,
- Who you surround yourself with,
- Who you choose to follow,
- How you perform in moments of crisis or opportunity,
- How you interact with team members,
- The organization's strategy,
- Your own mind-set,
- Timing,
- And many other factors.

## IT'S NOT PERSONAL

I learned this lesson—and many others—the hard way. Too often, I was attached to the things that happened. I took the disappointments personally. I questioned why people didn't think I was "good enough."

I focused my anger in ways that had no productive results and did nothing but make me unhappy. At times, because of my reactions, I probably caused people to give me a wide berth when I could have used more friends.

As you'll read in the chapters dedicated to telling other real career stories, it's pretty common to take things that happen to us personally, when in reality, it's "just business." In some cases, employees are laid off not because they weren't providing value, but because the company's strategy changed or due to economic factors that negatively impacted business.

### ACCESSING YOUR POWER

When we step back from feeling like a change is personal, it enables us to have more access to the energy required to recover and move on. When we stay mired in feeling like a victim, not only are we wasting time we could be spending on what's next, but we can also repel people who could help us find that next opportunity.

My objective with this book is to share my own stories and the stories of some interesting and accomplished professionals—the funny ones, the depressing ones, the happy ones, and even the humiliating ones. If even one person learns something from my experiences and those of the people I interviewed, then the mishaps will have been worth it.

### WAKING UP TO FIND YOUR JOB ISN'T A FIT

I've coached many mid-career professionals whose primary goal getting out of college was to get a job—really any job. They wanted to start making money and making a career for themselves without much thought about their passions and strengths. High-achieving people are typically able to do a lot of things, and often they just look for someone willing to exchange money for tasks they can do. This is a common theme in several of the career stories in the book.

Fast forward ten or twenty years, and they can find themselves "successful" in a career they actually didn't consciously choose and which may not be a great fit for them. Even if you don't like your job, it can be tough to leave, especially if you're highly compensated and your lifestyle is based on that income.

Several of the people I interviewed in the book had similar experiences and were able to reevaluate what they loved to do and were good at, then find a fit between those skills that they enjoyed using and the needs within the marketplace.

## UNDERSTANDING THE BALANCE OF POWER

Workers sometimes feel that the employer holds all the cards and that they, as employees, have little control over the path of their careers. It can really depend on the situation, but often the employees have much more control than they recognize.

The reality is that employers need employees to create the value that their customers buy. While not every organization is this enlightened, the best employers recognize that aligning their employees' skillsets and passions with the needs of the business increases employee engagement, productivity, and innovation, which benefits the company and their customers.

## HOW CAREER CONTRIBUTES TO IDENTITY

Though you might still have a hard time looking at work as a game, its distinct advantage has to do with how closely we associate our jobs with our identities. Much like when I didn't get the promotion at my first job and felt betrayed, many people can get attached to things that happen at work. Our judgment can become clouded with emotion.

The actions and outcomes may or may not have anything to do with us personally, but nevertheless, we can take them that way. Strong emotions lead to all kinds of actions that can be a problem at work, from losing control—think crying or yelling—to holding grudges that don't make for a happy or productive work environment.

## ROLL THE DICE AND PLAY THE GAME

When you think of your work situation as a game, it helps to remove you from the "day-to-day" as you gain a broader perspective and see the whole game board. Your boss, company leaders, peers, direct reports, and customers are the players. You can observe the dynamics of how various players interact with each other and choose how you'd like to play. The goal is to recognize that your *perception* of the events is what gives them meaning. When you see things from a different perspective, the meanings can begin to change as well.

Roll the dice and start playing the game of work!

## CHAPTER 2

# WHAT KIND OF PLAYER ARE YOU?
## Getting to Know Yourself

———

*At the center of your being you have*
*the answer; you know who you are*
*and you know what you want.*

—LAO TZU[7]

In my work as an executive coach, people often tell me they aren't satisfied with where they are currently, yet have a hard time articulating what would make them happy. From the outside, they seem extraordinarily successful with impressive titles, six-figure incomes, and résumés full of significant accomplishments. I'll ask, "What do you want?" and many times, I'll get a forlorn response. "I don't know."

---

7    Lao Tzu Quotes. Goodreads.com. Accessed January 25, 2020.

## JUMPING THROUGH HOOPS

People who succeed in the business, academic, or nonprofit worlds typically have jumped through a lot of hoops to get to the level of success they enjoy—a college education, oftentimes an advanced degree, and years of work experience. They've paid their dues working their way up the ladder.

They have been programmed over the years to be sensitive to the expectations of those around them. Each successive phase of their journey required proving themselves. In my practice, I encounter many experienced professionals who are highly successful by external measures but are not satisfied inside.

## EXCESSIVE FOCUS ON EXTERNAL CUES

One such client is Bill. He is Ivy League–educated with an MBA from a top-ten business school. He is employed by a blue-chip firm in a role in which he's successful and well paid, yet he wonders what his real purpose is.

He followed the directions that many parents and guidance counselors point to as the ideal path for bright and accomplished high school students—leverage your intellect, extracurricular accomplishments, and strong work ethic to gain admittance into a top university, then parlay that into a postgraduate degree from a top school, then get a high-paying job with a corporation. Like Bill, many students are told that after their ticket is punched, they'll be recruited by employers seeking the best and brightest.

With this formula, many people achieve high levels of professional success as measured by their accomplishments, level of responsibility, and income. What I often see is that many will follow this well-worn path faithfully without stopping to check in with themselves. They may never even contemplate what their ultimate goal is and whether, once attained, it will bring them satisfaction. In fact, they may have been so focused on external cues that they never asked themselves what they really want.

## LOSING TOUCH WITH ONESELF

It's common for the first call that I have with a potential client to go something like this:

**Professional:** I have a great job, and I'm successful where I am. In fact, I'm being considered for a promotion, but the only problem is I'm not sure I want it.

**Coach:** I see. What is it about the promotion that doesn't interest you?

**Professional:** Well, I'm good at what I do, and this would get me to the next level, but I don't enjoy it.

**Coach:** It makes sense that you might have some hesitation about taking the promotion if you don't enjoy the work. What type of work would you enjoy doing?

**Professional:** That's the problem. I don't even know what I'd enjoy doing. The things I'm interested in won't bring in the income that would support my lifestyle. I have a queasy feeling about taking this promotion, yet I don't think I have a choice. I feel like I should be happy, but I'm not.

**Coach:** If you're not happy, how would you feel about exploring a job where you'd be happier?

**Professional:** What I enjoy doing won't pay what I need to make, and I need to maximize what I earn to support my lifestyle. My peers are rising to this level, and I feel pressure to keep up if I want to have a successful career. I'll probably just take the job, and I figure maybe I can sock away the money and retire early. Then I'll do what makes me happy.

## THE TRAP OF HIGH ACHIEVEMENT

Tom DeLong is a Harvard Business School professor and author who has studied what he calls "high-need-for-achievement" types. He defines this group as "driven, ambitious, [and] goal oriented." DeLong observes that often these individuals become addicted to the success they've accomplished and expect that they will continue to enjoy the same level of success. They can become anxious and sometimes even frozen about the possibility of failing.[8]

---

8    DeLong, Thomas J. Flying Without a Net: Turn Fear of Change into Fuel for Success. Harvard Business Review Press, 2011. p. x (preface).

In an interview on HBR.com from May 2011[9], DeLong elaborated on this concept.

"They figured out that they had this drive. And I think they began to leverage it. And they also began to compete. And it's not just to be number one once or twice, but it's to be number one all the time. And so what happens gradually is that the external criteria for success becomes the norm. So we're not looking at our own talents and saying, how have I grown and developed these talents that I've realized over the years? I say, well, when I go to this five-year reunion, how am I going to compare with all those people that I competed with? And so it's that success is only defined in terms of how I do compared to other people. And that, in itself, becomes addictive and becomes its own pattern."

## ADDICTION TO EXTERNAL VALIDATION

As a coach, I've observed the pattern that DeLong describes with clients, and I've experienced it personally. High achievers can become so conditioned to reacting to external factors and measuring their success by what others say or think that they may even lose the ability to read their own internal cues that help them know what they want.

Like a compass can reverse polarity when a strong magnet is situated in its vicinity, this external focus becomes the magnet that pulls them away from knowing what their own

---

9    Sarah Green, "The Hidden Demons of High Achievers" interview with Thomas DeLong, HBR.com, https://hbr.org/2011/05/the-hidden-demons-of-high-achi, May 2011.

values and desires are. Essentially, they cease to relate to their own definition of success—if they ever even had one.

Like my client, Bill, it can be a slow and delicate process helping "high-need-to-achieve" types discover their own desires. First of all, they may become so accustomed to seeking the approval of others that their ability to rely on their own judgment may be underdeveloped. Secondly, their success has been predicated on their ability to delay gratification as they pursue education or "pay their dues" to rise within their profession.

They receive rewards for this ability to suppress their immediate desires, and at some point, they actually become addicted to the rewards gained from that suppression. They feel discomfort and a sense of unease because those innate and unique desires still exist, but they have developed habits to become "successful." An internal tug-of-war is usually the discomfort that drives people to seek help in sorting it out.

### UNEARTHING INTERNAL CUES
A lot of blocks are caused by high achievers' accumulated beliefs that need to be examined and either consciously embraced or replaced. It's as if one's true desires were an internal spring that has been paved over. Occasionally, a trickle of water will make its way through the pavement, but it's not easy to find the source. As one does the work to remove what blocks it, the flow becomes stronger.

At the beginning of this rediscovery process, it's critical to take note of sensations in the body as you experience them:

- Is there a tightness in the stomach or a fluttery, exciting feeling in the chest?
- Are you having a hard time getting out of bed in the morning when certain activities are planned for the day, or are you leaping out of bed with energy to spare?
- Are your shoulders tense or relaxed?
- Do you find yourself clenching your jaw or sighing regularly?
- Notice your resting facial expressions.
- Are your brows furrowed and mouth tight when you undertake certain activities?
- Or is your face relaxed with the corners of your mouth slightly upturned toward a smile?

## TAPPING INTO THE WISDOM OF THE BODY

As you notice these bodily sensations, take a moment to stop and take note of the situations that elicit particular responses. Your body has a wisdom of its own. Unfortunately, too often we choose to ignore the wisdom of the body and instead rely only on the one-dimensional, logical intelligence of the mind.

The mind can focus and rationalize, which can be valuable at times, but when you allow the mind to be the primary driver in your life, you may ignore the wisdom of your body, emotions, and intuition. All are legitimate sources of information and truth about ourselves and others.

On mornings when you have a hard time getting out of bed for work or have indigestion before going to a particular meeting, stop and ask yourself the following questions. They can also provide a helpful guide for journaling if you're not feeling in touch with your true desires:

- What is my thought right now?
- What is this feeling?
- Where is this coming from?
- What choices do I have? (Even if I choose not to make one of these choices.)
- What is the belief that is causing me to choose this action?
- How true is this belief?
- What would happen if I believed something different?
- What would I need to do to experience this situation differently?

Go through a similar process when you find yourself feeling energized and excited. Ask:

- What is my thought right now?
- Which of my values is this aligning with?
- What about this excites me?
- How did this come about?
- How can I experience more of these types of situations?
- What beliefs hold me back from experiencing this more?

## UNTANGLING YOUR DESIRES

When my clients are rediscovering their passions, where they derive their energy and purpose, it's like pulling a red thread from a tangled ball of multicolored thread. You may see the red thread twisted among the others, but it's hard to pull only the red thread out. You may need to untwist and unknot some clusters to free the red thread. It can take some work, but once you've seen the thread, you know what your objective is and can get to work freeing it from the snarl.

## UNLEARNING PROGRAMMING

Young children don't usually have much problem asking for what they need. During roughly the first seven years of life, they are unselfconscious. If they feel hurt, they'll cry. If they're happy, they'll express their joy by laughing, running around, jumping, and more. If they are curious, they'll blurt out their question no matter the situation. As we grow older, we internalize the message that we need to have more control over our natural emotional responses.

We get messages from parents and in school about what acceptable behavior is and is not. Over time, the reinforcement of certain behaviors and punishment or disincentives around "undesirable" behavior can cause people to disconnect from their emotions. With this repression, it can be difficult to discern what makes us happy.

## ASKING FOR WHAT YOU REALLY WANT

Sometimes, going back to those childhood memories can help us get back in touch with that part of ourselves. When I was a little kid, I got so excited when Christmas was coming. I would lay in the middle of the living room floor flipping through every page of the Sears catalog, circling all the things I wanted, and then I'd faithfully transcribe each item into a letter to Santa.

As a child at Christmas, I had no guile or sophistication, only hope and faith that Santa Claus would bring me what I wanted for Christmas. I didn't temper my desires then. I asked for an Appaloosa pony and tree house even when my family lived in a trailer on a rented lot with no trees big enough for a tree house. I didn't worry about the practicalities. I knew what I wanted, and I had the faith to ask for it and believe that my dream could come true.

## GETTING BACK IN TOUCH WITH YOURSELF

To get in touch with your innermost desires and what makes you happy, think back to your childhood. These questions can help you discover the connection to your authentic self:

- What were you excited by as a child?
- What did you want to be when you grew up? What was exciting for you about that?
- Are the answers you came up with focused on people, ideas, concepts, data, things, or some combination?
- Did you like playing with others or by yourself as a child?
- If you're doing something different now than you wanted to do as a child, at what point did you change paths?
- Did your change of paths happen because you decided yourself or was it based on someone else's input or feedback?
- What regret, if any, do you have about not following this childhood dream?
- In one small way, how can you honor your childhood ambition?

## SEEING THE FOREST FOR THE TREES

While focus on your goals can be helpful, hyper-focus on a specific opportunity can narrow your perspective to prevent you from seeing when the goal is within your grasp, perhaps because it looks different than your preconceived notion. In her excellent and inspiring book, *You are a Badass,* Jen Sincero[10] shares an example that illustrates this perfectly:

> There's a great Hindu story about a lady who wanted to meet the god Krishna. She went into the forest, closed her eyes, and prayed and meditated on making the god appear, and lo and behold, Krishna came wandering down the forest path toward her. But when Krishna tapped the lady on the shoulder, she, without opening her eyes, told him to get lost because she was busy meditating on an important goal.

How many times, like this lady, have you asked for something, been presented with what you requested, but didn't recognize it because it was in a different package than what you expected? You may have been so focused on what you thought it should look like that the object of your desire passed right under your nose. In reality, you could be lamenting your bad luck when you are simply blind to the riches that surround you.

---

10    Sincero, Jen. *You are a Badass: How to Stop Doubting Your Greatness and Start Living an Awesome Life.* Running Press, 2013. p. 39.

## IS YOUR GOAL ACTUALLY *YOUR* GOAL?

Most of us are guilty of this on some level. You may decide on a goal for all the wrong reasons. Maybe you chose a goal because someone else wanted it for you, like becoming vice president by age thirty, because that's what dear old Dad did. Or maybe you pursue a certain profession because you think it will be lucrative or impress others.

Stella became a concert violinist because that's what her mother had been and she expected Stella to follow the same path. It wasn't her dream, but Stella had a great deal of success as a violinist, even though she didn't love it. Later in life, Stella left her career as a professional musician and began a career she loved based on her own desires.

For goals to be truly motivational, you've got to understand why you are pursuing them, and the reasons have to have real meaning for you. Like my violinist friend, you can be successful in a career that you don't like, but you probably won't be happy. So really, what's the point of success without happiness?

## WHEN LONG WAY GETS YOU THERE FASTER

As the maxim goes, "All roads lead to Rome." Many routes lead to the same destination. Don't get too caught up in thinking your goal is out of reach because you had to take a detour or are temporarily stalled. It's even okay to decide that you want to change your destination along the way. (After all, it is *your* life!)

Sometimes ambitious people refuse to take on volunteer or side projects because they are too "busy" with their jobs, and they view that sort of thing as just "meaningless busywork." This is analogous to someone who is stuck in a traffic jam on the highway refusing to get off and take side streets because they are convinced the highway is faster, despite evidence to the contrary.

People who volunteer or take on special projects outside their primary responsibilities often see their investments pay off in spades. They learn, grow their networks, and become more visible to leaders inside and outside their organizations, which can lead to bigger or more interesting roles. It's the result of stepping out and differentiating themselves from those who were just doing their job.

To continue with this metaphor, these people got off the highway, sat through a few lights on the side streets, then got a speedy police escort to their destination. Remaining present, centered, and open can enable you to see the myriad of ways to get from point *A* to point *B*.

## NAVIGATING THE "JUNGLE GYM"

Career advancement is no longer a linear march up the ladder—*if it ever was!* Today, it's more of a jungle gym with many routes that can lead to the next level. Many organizations commonly give emerging leaders assignments outside the normal hierarchy to gain broader perspectives and understanding so they can eventually rise to the executive level.

Sometimes the assignments can include being transferred to a different unit to work under a more experienced manager, moving from a line position to a staff position, or vice versa, or even being transferred to another geographical location. The purpose of these meandering paths and the objective of such assignments is to provide these "high potentials" with exposure to a variety of challenges that will strengthen leadership muscles and prepare them for higher-level leadership roles.

Even if you don't work in the corporate world or aren't currently on the high-potential list, you can seek varied opportunities to round out your skillset and build your network of friends and colleagues who are willing to help you achieve your goals. Share your aspirations. Talk to people who do what you'd like to do. Ask for what you want. Reach out to organizations doing work that interests you and see what opportunities exist.

## FINDING NEW PATHS

If you hold on too tightly to the idea that you have to do everything yourself and that you'll never catch a break— guess what? You won't! Each time you move out of your comfort zone, you stretch, learn, and grow. When you find the courage to do this, you'll discover new paths that can lead to where you want to go.

Remain open . . . and who knows? You may wake up and realize that your dream is coming true right before your eyes—perhaps in a different way than you originally envisioned. That's okay though. The world is full of possibilities. The first step is figuring out what you want. Then, you have to stay open and alert to see the opportunities before you.


## HAVE THE COURAGE TO LISTEN TO YOURSELF

When you create an active dialogue with yourself, you will develop a better understanding of what makes you happy, and you will also begin to trust your instincts more. When the blocks have been removed from the spring of your desires, joy and fulfillment will become a more regular experience in your life and career.

**EXERCISE: DISCOVERING YOUR *WHY***

Here are some questions to ask to discover the *why* behind your goals. Get a notebook and write out the answers for yourself. Later, spend some time reading over your answers to see what you learned about yourself and your *whys*:

- How will you feel when you achieve this goal?
- What rewards will you gain by achieving this goal?
  - Money?
  - A sense of accomplishment?
  - A new title?
  - Higher self-esteem?
  - Continued opportunities for advancement?
  - Someone else's approval? (*This is a red flag!*)
- What will achieving this goal mean to you? To your family and friends?
- Does someone want this goal for you more than you want it for yourself? If so, how has that impacted your decision to pursue this goal?
- Would you still pursue the goal someone else wants for you if they were gone tomorrow?
- If you can access the feelings and rewards that you desire through other means, how willing are you to alter your goal or path to get there?

# HOLLY: DISCOVERING HER SUPERPOWER

———

Holly Segur is the president and CEO of a subsidiary of a Fortune 200 company. As a nontechnical leader in a scientific organization, her rise was extraordinary and based on a skillset that came so naturally to her that for a long time she didn't recognize it as special. Holly is also an executive coach and principal at Holly Segur Intuitive Healing.

As is often the case, the skills that come easiest for us are the ones that we can take for granted and assume everyone else also has. In Holly's case, her highly-attuned intuitive skills contributed significantly to her professional success, though it took her years to fully recognize it as her "superpower."

## IN HER OWN WORDS

I grew my career over twenty-four years from an entry-level role into a top executive position leading an organization of more than six-hundred people. I was able to advance to an executive level in about ten years. It wasn't a particular ambition of mine. It happened organically. People began to ask me to coach them because they wanted to learn the techniques that enabled me to rise so quickly.

### RECOGNIZING HER UNIQUE GIFT

At first, I would say, "Oh, I didn't really do anything. It just sort of came to me." As I got older, I realized that my reliance on intuition helped me to read people and situations and to understand the real dynamics of what was going on around me that might not be apparent to others. That was an advantage to me.

To be an effective leader, you don't necessarily need book smarts. You have to have good people skills, which came naturally to me. That success helped me realize the value of helping leaders tap into their intuition and their gut. It's not easy for everyone—for me, it was second nature.

### EMOTIONAL INTELLIGENCE IS NOT INHERENT

People who have grown in their career based on technical expertise don't always know how to lead people. I recognized an opportunity to use my particular mentorship to help others combine intuitive leadership, technical expertise, and ambition.

I've helped managers and executives who lack the soft skills and the right-brain ability to get in touch with that inner wisdom and intuition. That's how I came to work as a coach—it was kind of an evolution of people asking me to help them—I was doing it for free at first, then I said to myself, "I could probably make some money doing this."

### HELPING OTHERS DEVELOP THEIR INTUITIVE SKILLS

Intuition is a skill that can be developed by almost anyone. Many leaders have shut off the connection to their intuition for a variety of reasons. They've defaulted to patterns of response to make decisions. I help them develop new patterns.

I push them to go inside themselves and get in touch with their intuition. I say, "You already know the answer. You've buried the answer under a lot of emotional filters." I'm constantly holding up a mirror and pushing clients to peel away the layers until they get to that "aha" moment.

For some, it takes only a few of those situations before they understand how to do it and can take it from there on their own. But I've had leaders who say, "I can't do this. It's just not my nature. I'm not that kind of person."

In many cases, they have shut off the connection to their emotional body as a survival mechanism. I use tools to help them talk about the experiences that caused them to be afraid of taking risks. The goal is to work through those past experiences to make sense of them.

## GETTING IN TOUCH WITH INTUITION

I love this work because every client and every situation is unique. I help people safely get back in touch with themselves and begin to feel their emotions. It's delicate because I don't want them to suddenly crash and go to a place where they become so emotional and empathic that they're paralyzed.

Some leaders in corporate environments put themselves in an almost-robotic state. It may be easier when they're in positions of authority to ignore their emotions and allow their intellect to lead. In these cases, when I ask what they want to do, they have a hard time getting in touch with their desires and needs because they've cut off that connection.

## THIS IS SCIENCE, NOT WOO-WOO STUFF

Everyone is born with the capacity to use their intuition, yet I've encountered some skepticism about the importance of intuition in the corporate world. I work with a lot of engineers and scientists who are really brilliant, technical people, but their capacity for accessing their soft side is almost nonexistent.

To overcome the skepticism, I share a lot of research around physics and energy. Working in a scientific organization, most of these folks understand physics on some level, and I point out that physics is about something they can't see or touch—and that this is the same thing.

I'll often share the work of Dr. Joseph Dispenza, who has written a lot on blending quantum physics with the science of the mind-body connection. When I share the science around this, I find there's much more acceptance.

When I pull up legitimate sources, people are sometimes astonished and say, "Okay, you're not just making this up?"

I assure them, "No, I'm not just some woo-woo freak. It's science. It's real."

**BEING INTUITIVE IN AN ANALYTICAL ORGANIZATION**
It took me a good year after I started my coaching practice to be willing to talk about my reliance on intuition, because some people were giving me the side-eye and asking, "What's this woman's deal? What do you mean intuition?"

So many people in the company, if you were to put them side by side with me, have fancy degrees from MIT or Harvard, and all I have is a state university degree. They were hired as fabulous scientists with innovations and patents. I'm just a person relying on this natural ability. It can sometimes feel like that's not enough.

In a structured environment, people can sometimes give my intuitive skills a sideways glance. I know this is the real deal, and I need to stand firm in it. Those were the mental steps that I had to take to reinvent myself and change the structured, formal, mainstream corporate executive I had been for so many years.

**WHEN PEOPLE FEEL TRAPPED IN THEIR CAREERS**
My ideal clients are the ones who have it all but *don't.* They're the ones who are successful but not satisfied. They're confused

about why their life isn't perfect. They've done everything they were taught to do. And yet, they feel empty.

When clients feel stuck in their careers, I really encourage them to talk about something bigger than themselves. I'll remind them that they've done what they needed to do, and perhaps their work there is done. They need to find something else. If they've built their entire career around this work, when things change naturally, they feel lost. It's not just about the job.

### FOLLOWING SOMEONE ELSE'S "RULES"

When people aren't happy in their careers, they are almost always following what they were told to believe. They have bought into limiting beliefs from their education, religion, and family life. They believe those rules determine what's right and what's wrong. They don't realize they're supposed to be on a completely different path. They're unhappy because they're living according to someone else's expectations.

Oftentimes, they don't even know their own expectations for themselves. I give them permission to let go of everything from their past . . . to let go of the fact that their parents spent a ton of money on their PhD when that's not really what they wanted to do. I help them figure out what they want. We examine what they want to let go of and what they want to bring forward that doesn't exist in their life today.

### UNDOING EARLY PROGRAMMING

It goes back to childhood programming. If their life is going to change, the beliefs that brought them to their current state have to be undone. Success depends on their willingness to let go of those beliefs. As a coach, it's most satisfying when clients can say, "I don't have to believe everything that I was told. I can let go of these beliefs. In some parts of my life, I'm willing to say I can do something different." It's really powerful.

This change requires clients to constantly challenge their own way of thinking. It can be terrifying to step away from long-held beliefs and envision their life without those rules. If someone is used to following the rules and suddenly they're a rule breaker, it feels scary. As a coach, I give my clients permission to let that go. From there, they can visualize and create their future reality.

## OVERCOMING INTERNAL AND EXTERNAL HURDLES
Everybody has a different definition of success. Early on for me, success was about the title and income. When I achieved that, I shifted to serve a greater purpose and answer the question around *why* I do what I do.

A big victory for me was being confident enough to become myself. It's natural to compare myself to others, but it's not really helpful. Even if two people are in the same role, they're not the same. Different people have different perspectives and experiences and therefore respond to challenges differently and create different outcomes. It was a hurdle for me to accept that about myself. I recognize that what I accomplished is good enough, so I don't have to compare myself to others. For me, that's been huge.

### THE RESULTS SPEAK FOR THEMSELVES

I live close to Cornell University and a couple of other Ivy League colleges. When I talk to people about coaching, I often get the question, "What are your credentials? What's your background? What are your certifications?"

I have to share that I don't have any credentials in coaching. I'm intuitive but have worked as a coach for thirteen years. I can share my metrics for my corporate work in terms of the size of my organization and the kind of initiatives and turnarounds that I've performed.

### NO CERTIFICATION NEEDED

I have the technical experience, but I don't have a professional certification in coaching. It's been another mental hurdle for me. The demon of imposter syndrome makes me feel like I have to have all sorts of professional certifications.

I have to tell myself no. I don't really need that. I'm selling what I have right now. I'm happy to tell clients about my coaching track record, and I'm happy to teach them, but I don't come with certificates on the wall, nor am I interested in getting them. Accepting myself gave me confidence and enabled me to recognize I'm good enough just the way I am.

### ADVICE FOR BEING HAPPY AT WORK

This is not about other people making you happy. If you can be anything you want to be, are you prepared to change your mindset? Are you prepared to take ownership of your happiness? Are you ready to fill your own cup? Are you prepared to do the work? If you can answer yes to these questions, you can do anything, because happiness at work requires changing the way you think about a situation, identifying what you need, and getting help. It's about adjusting your mind-set for the situation and seeing the possibilities.

It's possible for anyone. They may need some coaching to learn to manage their mind-set. People know how to complain, gossip, and judge. When we learn to be positive, we can turn around any situation and find happiness, joy, and gratitude. That's a beautiful place to be.

## EXERCISE: WHAT'S YOUR SUPERPOWER?

As Holly leaned into her innate gifts, she became more successful. From a place of authenticity, each of us can find a more natural fit within the workforce. To help you recognize and develop your own gifts and intuition, spend some time writing out answers to these questions:

- What abilities make you different?
- Do you acknowledge these unique abilities as gifts?
- How comfortable are you with sharing your gifts?
- In what situations do you find yourself hiding your gifts? What do you fear?
- How often and under what circumstances do you listen to or ignore your intuition?
- In what environments do you feel most authentic?
- When you think of revealing more of the "real you" at work, how do you feel?
- What would need to happen for you to show up more authentically at work? What are the pros and cons of this?
- Write about a time when you were the most authentically "you" at work. What happened? What lesson did you take away from that experience? Has it helped or hurt you at work?
- How concerned are you about what people will think of you if you show up just as you are?

## CHAPTER 3

# WHAT'S YOUR OBJECTIVE? Figuring out What You Want

---

*Have the courage to follow your heart and intuition. They somehow already know what you truly want to become. Everything else is secondary.*

—STEVE JOBS[11]

## WHY IS CARLA BREAKING THE RULES?

Ella had a demanding management role within a fast-moving industry. She scheduled a coaching call with me in the hope

---

11  Jobs, Steve. Prepared text of the Commencement address at Stanford University, June 12, 2005. Stanford.edu.

of gaining some clarity in a troubling situation at work. Ella shared several instances where her colleague and peer, Carla, had taken actions that bothered her.

Ella was angry and indignant that Carla had done these things with seemingly no concern for her. I listened and did what I was trained to do as an executive coach. I acknowledged and validated Ella's feelings. It was natural for her to feel anger and betrayal over some of Carla's actions.

As she calmed down, I tried to steer the conversation back to what Ella wanted to get out of the session, but that always seemed to bring us back to an "unfair" action that Carla had taken. Finally, I stopped her and asked, "Ella, I understand that you are bothered by Carla's actions. However, you will never be able to control Carla. You can only decide what actions you want to take. I'm going to ask you a direct question, and I'd like you to take a few moments to think it over before you answer. What is it that you want?"

That direct question seemed to stop Ella in her tracks. She made sort of a "hrumph" sound and was silent. Ella was so focused on Carla's actions and the emotion that they stirred in her, she hadn't stopped to understand why Carla's actions bothered her and what she needed to do to feel better.

## OWNING YOUR EMOTIONS

Ella said that Carla "made her mad." It's common to blame other people for our own emotional response; however, it's a fallacy. Ella was abdicating responsibility for her own happiness by allowing herself to be bothered by Carla's actions.

She had a belief about that situation which she could choose to change anytime.

Carla was likely not even aware that Ella was bothered by her actions. Ella did not end up hiring me after that first call, and she didn't share the reason why. My guess is that she was not ready to recognize the power she possessed to create a different reality than the one she was experiencing.

I would have loved to have helped her step fully into her own power so that she never again worried about what Carla was up to. I think we could have gotten there, but coaching only works when people commit to it and are ready to take action to change their own circumstances.

## BEHAVIORAL THEORY

Now is a good time to provide a little background on cognitive behavioral theory as developed by Dr. Aaron T. Beck in the 1960s[12]. When you enter a situation that reminds you of something you've previously encountered, the stimulus will trigger a thought or belief. Based on that thought, you'll have an emotional response, and based on that response, you'll take a certain action. The results of the action will serve as either a reward or a disincentive and will cause that response to be positively or negatively reinforced—meaning if it was rewarded, you'll be open to it happening again, and if it wasn't, you'll probably avoid it[13].

---

12   "A History of Cognitive Behavioral Therapy." Beckinstitute.com. Downloaded January 25, 2020.

13   Beck, J.S. Cognitive Behavior Therapy: Basics and beyond (2nd ed.). The Guilford Press, 2011. Pp. 19-20

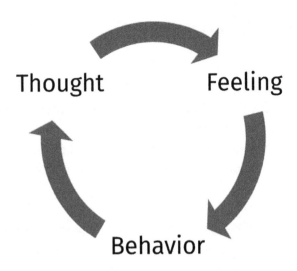

Thought      Feeling

Behavior

**YOU HAVE CONTROL OVER YOUR RESPONSES**

If you want to change this cycle, the optimal place to change it is at the belief or thought step. When you believe differently, you feel differently and take different actions. Here's an example of how this works:

> **Situation:** Car swerves into your lane on the highway, causing you to slam on the brakes.
>
> **Thought:** That driver purposely tried to endanger me.
>
> **Emotion:** Fear and anger.
>
> **Behavior:** Lay on the horn, speed up, and angrily shake your fist at the driver as you pass.

Here's the same scenario with a different thought:

**Situation:** Car swerves into your lane on the highway, causing you to slam on the brakes.

**Thought:** That driver must be in a big hurry. Maybe he's on his way to the hospital.

**Feeling:** Empathy and concern.

**Behavior:** Deep breath. Regain composure after surprise. Slow down and give him room to merge into your lane.

## KNEE-JERK REACTIONS

You may not even be aware of it because it happens so quickly. It becomes a knee-jerk reaction meaning that you respond to a stimulus without thinking: Car slams on brakes, subconscious belief (he's trying to hurt me), emotional response (fear, anger), conditioned response (hit the horn and yell).

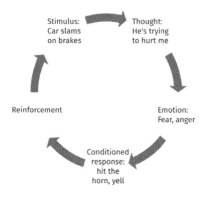

## ELLA'S BELIEFS

Ella's beliefs caused her to be angered by Carla's actions. Perhaps when Ella was a child, her parents instilled in her that one should always ask permission before taking action. Perhaps Carla's habit of taking action and informing Ella later conflicted with her belief that one should ask for permission. So here's an outline of what Ella's behavioral cycle might look like:

> **Situation:** Carla and Ella are working on a joint project. Carla takes an action and lets Ella know about it after the fact.
>
> **Ella's Belief:** When people work together, they should ask for permission before taking a step.
>
> **Feeling:** Anger that Carla is not following the "rules."
>
> **Behavior:** Complains about Carla. Lingering feelings of resentment toward her.

## CARLA'S BELIEFS

Carla likely has different beliefs than Ella, and because they haven't shared those beliefs about working together on projects, they have conflict. Perhaps Carla was raised by parents who expected their children to be autonomous and didn't expect them to ask for permission.

Because her beliefs are different than Ella's, she would see no need to ask Ella whether it was okay to take the next step in the project. The difference in their experiences and belief systems caused them to respond differently to the same situation.

The reason why it can be difficult to change behavior is that most of the time only a split-second passes between the trigger event, your brain's connection to a thought or belief, and the associated habitual response.

## ELLA'S OWN DESIRES

Ella was unable to tune in to what she really wanted out of her work situation. My guess is that she actually had some beliefs which kept her from acknowledging her own desires. Perhaps she felt work only was about focusing on the needs of the business and her boss's expectations. This belief would be in conflict with her acknowledging her own desires. Part of what was bothering her about her interactions with Carla could have been that Carla was focused on doing the things Ella wanted to do.

## HOW YOUR ENVY CAN HELP YOU

It is actually pretty common for people who I coach to have a hard time getting in touch with what they want. They know they aren't happy, but they don't know how to change their situation. I have found that taking note of another emotion that arises can help uncover what they really want. That emotion is envy.

Most people don't like to admit they're envious, yet it's something that we all feel at one time or another. Envy arises when you wish you had something that someone else has. It happens frequently in the workplace.

Sometimes it happens when a colleague gets a promotion or plum assignment that you wanted. Or it could crop up when a coworker contributes a great idea in a meeting or does a masterful presentation, and you say to yourself, "Wow, I wish I could do that."

### ENVY CAN LEAD TO JUDGMENT

In Ella's case, her anger may have actually been triggered by the underlying emotion of envy. Perhaps Ella subconsciously wanted the freedom Carla had when she took action without asking permission. When you feel envy, your subconscious is trying to tell you, "I'd like to do that too!" But conflict hits as another part of you is shutting that desire down fast because it seems dangerous or risky. The internal conflict is why it feels bad.

### TUG-OF-WAR BETWEEN DESIRES AND RISK

For years before I started my own business, I felt a sharp pang of envy when I saw people running their own businesses. I struggled for years to scratch my own entrepreneurial itch while working in big corporations. My appetite for risk and variety was appreciated by my employers during times of change but were not needed in the same way when the business settled into a routine, say after a merger had been integrated.

When I thought about leaving a steady job, part of me was screaming, "Leave this civilized place and go run free in the wild," while another part was saying, "What about your 401(k) and health insurance?" For me, it took a while to feel comfortable making a leap to become a full-time entrepreneur.

## FACING YOUR FEARS

If you ever have similar internal arguments raging inside, take some time to figure out what's really going on there. Your heart and soul may be trying to tell you something your head doesn't want to hear. Often, we have ideas we don't allow ourselves to explore out of fear—fear that we'll fail, fear that we'll succeed, fear of change, fear of what people will say, or fear of who we'll be outside of the status quo.

Let your heart and soul tell you what they want. Those parts want you to have joy and meaning in your life. Your head is the rational overseer that wants to make sure you are safe. Envy arises when there's conflict between these parts of yourself.

## BALANCING YOUR HEART AND YOUR HEAD

When you allow the thoughts in your head to slam the door on the desires of your heart and soul, you're basically telling yourself that you don't deserve happiness or joy—that it's not even worth seeing if it would be possible to pursue your dreams.

Pay attention to what lies beneath when you feel those feelings. Ask yourself if you can pursue your dreams while also taking care of your practical needs. Often, we don't explore the things we want because our rational side shuts them down before we even begin.

And we keep feeling envy when someone else does what we'd really like to do, and we struggle on—not feeling the happiness and success that could be ours if we let ourselves be who we want to be. Next time you feel envy, invite it to sit for a while and tell you why it's there.

## EXPLORING OPTIONS ISN'T RISKY IN ITSELF

Sometimes you may find yourself shutting down options before they have time to rise to the level of consciousness. You may eliminate an idea because it's scary, "not practical," or even "impossible." But the reality is that you have infinite options. Each alternative comes with its own set of consequences, which you can decide to choose *(or not)*.

For example, sometimes, when new clients come to me, they'll say that they're unhappy with their jobs and that they wish they could quit, but they have "no choice" but to stay. I point out that it is a choice to stay, and they could also choose to leave.

Leaving would mean that they would no longer get their current paycheck, but that's a different issue. Sometimes, once they've recognized that leaving is an option (even if they choose not to select it) they actually feel better.

To illustrate, someone may feel claustrophobic and trapped in a tiny, windowless office on the tenth floor, but if they're then given the same size office down the hall with a window to the outside, they feel better. The space is the same, but they can now see that they aren't trapped. With some effort, they can get out into the world they see through their window. They may never choose to leave their office during the day, but the feeling of being trapped lessens.

Paying attention to envy is a hack that can enable you to see what you really want. As times change, your beliefs about how to get along in your world under present circumstances may not evolve, and that may leave you feeling as if you have no options. Like the tiny office, it's not necessarily the situation that causes the pain that leads to your dissatisfaction—it's your belief about the situation that causes it.

## CAREER NOSTALGIA CAN KEEP YOU STUCK

Similarly, if you've had great success and satisfaction in your job or company, you may expect that you'll continue to have the same type of satisfaction even as the circumstances evolve around you. You may feel discomfort but don't change anything because you've told yourself, "I like my job," or "There are a lot of great growth opportunities at this company," even as your restlessness grows.

Have you had times in your career where everything came together perfectly for a while? And do you look back longingly? I've experienced it a few times when I had great jobs with important and meaningful projects and great perks, working alongside smart coworkers and appreciative bosses. During those times, I was happy but probably didn't relish the moment as much as I could have.

## THE PERFECT SUMMER JOB

One summer break while I was in college, I waited tables at a trendy waterside restaurant that attracted a well-heeled crowd in search of relaxation on the beach during the days and dinners out with friends in the evenings.

It was a dream summer job. I'd lounge on the beach during the day and work in the late afternoons. The shifts were busy and went fast. The tips were generous and all cash. The young crew of fellow servers, bartenders, and cooks shared my goals of making money and having as much fun as we could pack into the summer.

After the restaurant closed most nights, the staff would make our way en masse to the bar next door to drink and dance. My halcyon days of summer, as always, soon ended. August rolled around, and I headed back to school.

I returned the following summer hoping for a repeat of the fun and excitement of the previous year, but the vibe just wasn't the same. It just felt like a good summer job rather than an exciting adventure.

## SLOWLY SLIPPING AWAY

We can't always see how wondrous the moment is until the invisible factors that make it perfect start slipping away—a new boss comes, a valued coworker moves on, budget constraints are implemented, or the economy takes a dip. I bring this up not to make you nostalgic about the good old days, but to point out that sometimes the planets are aligned and everything is perfect, but as things change, we can sometimes stay in a job out of habit, subconsciously waiting for the good times to come back.

Like lightning striking the same place twice, this rarely happens. Recognize the circumstances changing around you and make intentional decisions about your own career path rather than simply going with the flow.

## FINDING YOUR WAY

If you have experienced times when work was perfect and that's no longer the case, what are you doing now? Don't wait around to see if those good times return. If you've had even one of those moments, thank your lucky stars for it, cherish your blessings, and go find your next one.

Don't sit around hoping it will find you, because it won't. Get out and do something . . . network, find a mentor, go back to school, ask for more responsibility. Whatever you do, don't wait for it, because lightning doesn't strike the same place twice.

## TRUSTING YOURSELF

We're all born with an innate sense of what is right for us. It's just that, in the course of growing up and becoming socialized, we sometimes get disconnected from our own inner wisdom. Taking the time to reconnect with your own intuition and desires will serve you well both in your career and in your life. It's well worth the effort and may well be one of the most fulfilling things you ever do.

## EXERCISE: DISCOVER WHAT YOU WANT

In a notebook or journal, go to a quiet place where you have time to think. Write out the answers to these questions. Try not to edit yourself as you go through this process. You'll have time later to make decisions about which of your options you'd like to pursue.

- What did you want to be when you were a child?
- What did you love about it?
- If money were no option, what would you do?
- What things are easy for you?
- What do people tell you that you're good at?
- In what situations do you find yourself feeling envious?
- When you do things that you don't like to do, what motivates you to do them anyway?
- List at least three accomplishments that you're most proud of (personal or professional). What do they have in common?
- Take note of the times at work when you get angry or frustrated. At those times, take a moment to explore what your underlying thought or belief is. Write it down.
- Take note of times at work when things don't seem fair. Stop and see if you can identify your underlying belief that leads to that feeling. Write it down.
- Think about five people who are doing jobs that you'd love to do. (Don't worry about whether you're qualified at this point to do the job.)

- What about those jobs is attractive? Reach out to those five people and see if they would be willing to let you interview them about their jobs.
- When you ask yourself what you'd ideally like to do, are you able to admit your desires easily? Or do you find yourself coming up with reasons why you can't have what you want? Write down the excuses you come up with.
- What were the circumstances that led you to pursue the career you did? Were you following a dream or did you fall into it?
- Was there someone that encouraged you to take your path? Write down the story of how you came into your current job or career.

## CREATING YOUR ROAD MAP

Once you're clear on what you'd like to do for a living, answer these questions to help you develop a road map on how to get there. If you like your current career but want to be happier doing it, you can also use these questions to design a path to get there.

- What are the gaps between where you are and where you'd like to be? (Think training, location, connections, knowledge, money, etc.)
- How can you learn more about how to bridge some of these gaps? (It may be that you don't know what you don't know. You may need to do some research to learn where you can gather information that will help you learn more.)

- Who can tell you more about the job you think you'd like to do? If you don't know anyone directly, perhaps you know someone who can introduce you to someone. You can also look for forums of like-minded people on Facebook or LinkedIn where you may be able to get your questions answered. Alumni networks are a perfect place to look for people to reach out to.
- Do a Google search for your desired role. Check job listings for requirements of the role you would like to do. See if there are YouTube videos. Ask questions on Quora.

# SCOTT:
# IN PURSUIT
# OF PASSION AND
# EXCELLENCE

———

Scott Wentworth is the CEO and founder of Wentworth Financial Communications, a marketing communications agency that develops thought leadership and other marketing content for financial services firms.

Scott's passion for his craft helped him to overcome the fears he had about leaving a comfortable corporate job to found his agency and has helped him face the challenges that come with being a business owner.

**IN HIS OWN WORDS**

I didn't start my career by searching for what could make me the most money. And I never cared about titles. Instead I was focused on, "What is the thing that I think I could be really great at?" That was always front and center. I didn't want to do something that I was just going to be okay at.

## CREATING A CAREER THAT FIT ME

In college, I was an economics major. I also took a lot of rhetoric, literature, and history classes. I liked doing research and putting all the pieces together to tell a story. That's the first time I remember liking writing.

After college, I began a yearlong internship in Springfield at the Illinois state legislature doing legal research and developing reports for legislators. Though I did not like legal research, I enjoyed the process of putting it all together and writing reports.

I had considered law school, but after that experience, I decided to get my master's in journalism at Northwestern University. I enjoyed finance and economics and wondered how I could combine these two things in my career. The folks in career services at Northwestern told me about corporate communications. I thought it sounded intriguing.

I applied for some jobs and got an internship at an investment bank as a part-time copywriter. I didn't even know what investment banking was at the time, but here I was working at one twenty hours a week. After graduation, I was hired full time as the deputy for the head of public relations and media relations handling media requests. It was a great experience and a good way to learn the industry.

I volunteered every time an opportunity to write came into the marketing department. I carved out a niche and eventually, I became the de facto head writer. I finally figured out what I enjoyed doing.

## FIRING ON ALL CYLINDERS

I longed to do something that I was passionate about where the actual skill of my craft mattered. I'm happiest when my job makes me feel like I'm firing on all cylinders. I felt like I was made to be a writer. It just feels natural.

Writing for financial services may not be the most exciting subject, but I'm totally engaged and energized doing it. Before doing this job, I never considered how thought leadership content was created. It seemed like the brochures and newsletters I received fell out of the sky into my mailbox.

I like the creativity involved in writing. I view writing white papers like a puzzle. I interview people to gather information, then I have to organize the ideas, creating order out of chaos. I'm not writing flowery, beautiful sentences. This is not literature. Instead, the creativity involves structuring ideas in a way that is interesting and understandable.

## THE ROAD NOT TAKEN

At one point, some folks at the firm suggested I look into becoming a financial advisor. They said, "You're personable. You have the math and people skills. You could do it." I would have liked developing relationships with clients, but I didn't think I could be any better at that job than most people, so I didn't pursue it.

I want to do something where I can be the best. What I do for a living has to be something that I really care about. The income and the lifestyle matter, but they are outcomes, not motivators, for me.

## A UNIQUE MARKETPLACE OPPORTUNITY

I worked at the bank for eleven years. About six or seven years into my tenure there, I sensed an opportunity in the marketplace. Financial services firms were doing more content marketing and thought leadership, and many firms were not large enough to have a dedicated writer on staff.

People told me, "You're a good writer. It's rare to find a good writer who understands marketing and also understands the technical side of financial services." That got me thinking, well, this company has eleven-hundred employees and only one writer in the marketing department.

Everyone was dealing with the challenge of how to develop the content. I did some research, talked to people within financial services marketing, and realized that I could meet a growing demand. That was when I first got the idea to start my business.

## LETTING GO OF GOOD ENOUGH

I made a hard decision to leave my job, and it took me several years to finally do it. Not only did I have great financial security there, but I knew exactly what was expected of me and I loved the people I worked with. If it hadn't been such a great place, it would have been a much easier decision to start my own company, and I probably would have done it much sooner.

One of the biggest hurdles to overcome was having the courage to walk away from a "good enough" job at the bank so that I could pursue possible greatness. I was driven by this intrinsic sense that I had to try to get to an ideal world. Even though it was good, something just felt incomplete in terms of my fulfillment. I felt like I was meant for something more than just "good enough."

**LAUNCHING MY BUSINESS**

I started Wentworth Financial Communications in 2015. My company is essentially a marketing agency. A lot of agency owners are similar to me in that they didn't set out to own a business. They set out to do their craft, then built the business around that.

I pulled the trigger and started the company the year after I got married. Being married and having my wife working in a corporate job with benefits made it easier.

People would say, "Oh, it was so brave of you to start a business. It must have been terrifying." Yes and no. Leaving something secure and jumping into this great unknown was a little scary, but it's a low-overhead business. It wasn't hard to be cash-flow positive.

Worst-case scenario: I'd give the business three years, and if it didn't work, I could go back to being an in-house writer for a bank. Fear and uncertainty was involved, but I tried to be logical—could I live with the worst-case scenario? The answer was a resounding yes.

### FOLLOWING MY PASSION AND PURPOSE

Challenge is part of the reason I love having my own company. There's always something new. At the investment bank every year, they had another end-of-the-year review. Back in 2011, I wrote it the best I could. What was really that different in 2012? My business, however, enabled me to feed my intellectual curiosity and enjoy the stimulation of new challenges.

Intellectual curiosity is one of my strongest values. I like learning and explaining things, and that is essentially what my job is. Even though my company is not an altruistic, mission-based company, what I do helps people. It's rewarding and motivating for me to know I'm helping a company and their people explain their ideas.

I know how frustrating it is when people have an idea and they can't get it out of their heads. Even when the ideas are clear in their heads, people can spend a lot of time agonizing over the writing, and even after all that effort, what they wrote doesn't really explain what they meant. I love alleviating that pain. It's what I was made to do.

### WHAT WOULD YOU DO FOR FREE?

I've tried to follow the advice to create a career around doing something that I love so much I'd do it for free. Here's a recent example:

My mom is on the property owners' association board in the community where my parents live. They were trying to pass a referendum, and she was writing an article for the community newsletter about why residents should vote to increase the property taxes by two-hundred dollars a year. She emailed me the draft article. Though it made sense, it was long, and it wasn't organized to maximize the impact of her argument.

Believe it or not, I enjoyed spending three hours on the phone on a Saturday working through how she could communicate this more clearly. I helped her articulate the message so readers would understand the referendum and any objections could be addressed in her article. I loved rewriting her article so that it was clear and impactful. It was fun and rewarding for me.

My philosophy is if you don't love what you do, why do it? I am pretty laser-focused on my tasks. When I decide to do something, I have to be all the way in to be happy. I'm not happy if I'm only halfway in.

## BEING AT THE CENTER OF THE ACTION

I want to be at the core of the business, not just a resource they bring in when they need it. Even though I'm doing the exact same thing in my business as I was doing at the bank, now I am on the management team.

I love being involved in the revenue-producing part of the company, the center of the action. I wanted to build something the way I thought it should be built and to have equity. Every day, I'm adding another brick to the building and that feels right for me.

## NO SLACK IN THE ROPE

Every decision I make is going to have a direct impact on the company, for better or worse. I'm not making decisions to satisfy someone above or below me or to navigate some internal review process. Every decision matters. There's no slack in the rope, which is nice, but it's also a burden.

*I can't say, "It's not my job."*

Every decision I make is going to affect the outcome of the company, and I have to be okay with that. I can't say, "It's not my job. I just did what they asked me to do. The ball's in someone else's court and I'm done." No more excuses. For me, it's energizing and also exhausting, because I have to think through things much more.

## MOVING TOWARD SOMETHING

Here's some advice for the would-be entrepreneur: don't go out and start a company because you don't like your current job. That's a bad reason to become an entrepreneur. Bad things are a part of whatever job you have. Don't move away from something. Instead, move toward something when you start a company.

Even though I couldn't imagine loving my current job more, there are some terrible parts about being a business owner. If you think the bad stuff is going to go away if you find the right job, you're kidding yourself. You'll just have other bad stuff to deal with at the new job.

## MY DEFINITION OF SUCCESS

I have my own definition of success. My dad is a farmer, and that has impacted how I think about business. Farming involves a lot of risk. My dad doesn't do it because it's a great way to make money. Money matters, but he does it because he loves it and wants to be great at it. I inherited that mindset and absorbed a lot from watching him work.

I'm one-hundred-percent happy with my decision to start the company. Professionally, it was the greatest decision I could have made. It's incredibly rewarding, but it's also the hardest thing I'll ever do. The highs are so much higher and the lows so much lower than they ever were before.

## MOVING FORWARD IN THE FACE OF FEAR

With stimulation sometimes comes fear. I must be aware of what is happening physiologically in my body when I am nervous, stressed, or scared. Being aware doesn't stop me from feeling that way, but if I understand what's happening, it makes it easier.

I'll take a breath and just let the feeling pass and come back to a level place. I've learned not to make decisions when my heart is racing or my palms are sweaty. Being present and being aware of what's going on is super helpful.

To anyone looking for a career that fits them better, don't let fear stop you from doing things you want to try. Just because you're scared doesn't mean you should stop doing the thing you want to do. Just keep going!

**EXERCISE: DISCOVERING YOUR PASSIONS**

Spend some time writing out answers to these questions:

- Does your current role fulfill you? If not, what do you need to do to increase your career satisfaction?
- What work-related activities would you do for free because you enjoy them so much?
- What opportunities exist at your workplace to do things you enjoy? How can you spend more time doing those things? Ask? Volunteer? Apply for another job?
- If you're not currently pursuing your professional passion, what blocks you from doing that? What steps can you take to get beyond these blocks?
- Where in your life are you settling for good enough instead of great?
- When you don't pursue the things you really want to do, what reason do you tell yourself? Is that reason really true?
- If you'd like to do something different, what can you do to reduce the risk of pursuing it?
- Can you honor your passion through volunteering or a hobby?

# PART 2

# LEARNING THE RULES OF THE GAME

## CHAPTER 4

# WHAT'S YOUR STRATEGY? Exploring Your Options

---

*Everything begins with an idea.*

—EARL NIGHTINGALE[14]

I've observed that people are unhappy with their jobs for a couple common reasons. Sometimes the unhappiness stems from a skill deficit that negatively impacts their effectiveness. At other times, the person may have the skills to do the job, but their unhappiness comes from something more innate—a lack of alignment between the job and their strengths, preferences, and values.

---

14 Economy, Peter. "37 Earl Nightingale Quotes That Will Empower You to Soar High." Accessed January 25, 2020.

## BRIDGING GAPS CAN BRING SATISFACTION

In the first scenario, identifying the gaps and developing the appropriate skills can help the person succeed and use their skills to meet expectations and feel confident. In the second situation, the person may be operating effectively but perhaps isn't aligned with the mission or culture of the organization and isn't motivated to perform in the role long term without significant stress and burnout.

When a person is unhappy with their job, it can sometimes be challenging to determine the root of the issue. At the heart of this dilemma is the big question: should I stay . . . or should I go?

## SHOULD I STAY OR SHOULD I GO?

I cannot consider that question without hearing the opening guitar riff from The Clash's punk rock anthem "Should I Stay or Should I Go" ringing in my ears. The lyrics illustrate the real pain of indecision. If you're not familiar with the song, look it up on YouTube. The song is not about breaking up with your job, but it certainly could be! The lyrics refer to a relationship that was exciting but had gotten stale. The relationship is at an inflection point—can it continue or is it time to break up?

When you started your new job, it was thrilling. Perhaps you were courted during the interview process before being singled out and offered the job. You probably felt lucky and special.

Then, maybe after being in the job for a while, things became a little more routine, some of the luster wore off, and that initial excitement started to fade away. After a few years, perhaps you rationalized the reasons for staying. But how do you know when it's time to go? Should you stay and see if things get better or jump ship?

## MISALIGNED EXPECTATIONS

I met Jason when he had been in his job with a small advisory firm for nearly twenty years and had risen through the ranks to chief administrative officer. He was the one who knew how everything worked, yet he'd recently been informed that he was not on a partner track. That was a huge blow to him and caused him to reconsider what his next career move would be.

For him, at age fifty, it was sobering to think about getting back in the job market, but with no growth opportunities on his current path, he also didn't think he could keep doing the same role for another fifteen years or more. He had mastered his role and couldn't find the motivation to continue if an ownership component wasn't in the cards.

## CALCULATING TRADE-OFFS

This is a tough place to be, yet many experienced professionals encounter this crossroad. They can stay with the same old familiar routine that pays well—where they know the company, have good benefits and a decent match on the 401(k), but what if staying drains their lifeblood? What if it causes stress and unhappiness?

I've spoken with many professionals as they've navigated this territory. Everyone must calculate their ideal ratio of happiness, stability, and fiscal rewards for the job. A question that many ask is:

*"Can I hold out for another three years? Five years? Ten years?"*

Staying can make sense from an economic standpoint. Leaving can also make sense from other perspectives. It's clearly a personal decision, but every professional must look at other factors such as health, relationships, and yes, happiness, to determine what the real trade-offs are.

Is it really smart to stay in a job that causes health issues? You've probably heard of people who have dropped dead on the job from a heart attack or were unhappy for a long time at work and developed cancer. These are extreme cases, but common enough to be taken into consideration if you're unhappy and under significant stress in your role.

## HAVING FAITH TO EXPLORE OPTIONS

Maybe a dream job exists where you could use your skills and interests in new and exciting ways—where you can continue to grow and explore. But if you've been in a role for a long time, even thinking that way can seem risky! How do you weigh the options?

Making a change may mean having to learn new systems and meet new people. For adults, the frustration of a new learning curve can be difficult to tolerate. Sometimes staying in a job that is familiar but unsatisfying may seem more attractive than facing the unknown, even if more happiness and engagement is the eventual result.

## LEARNING HOW TO LEARN AGAIN

As adults, we often aren't challenged to learn new things as often as children and younger adults. Learning new skills can be uncomfortable and can challenge our view of ourselves as competent and capable people.

We might assume that it's easier for younger people to learn, but a 2015 study done at the Interdisciplinary Graduate Program in Neuroscience at University of Iowa compared the learning ability of younger participants (average age of twenty-four) with older participants (average age of sixty-six) and found that the ability to learn "is largely unaffected by cognitive aging."[15]

Many older adults may not often be called on to learn new things in their jobs. This may lead them to rely on their existing knowledge out of habit rather than stepping out of their comfort zone to learn new skills. In other words, they can learn; they're just a little rusty.

To evolve and adapt to changing times, it's important to keep learning. If you can keep an open mind and not judge your-self when you're learning and haven't perfected something, you can maintain the energy to keep moving toward new goals.

---

15   Clark, Rachel, Michael Freedberg, Eliot Hazeltine and Michelle W. Voss. "Are There Age-Related Differences in the Ability to Learn Configural Responses?" https://journals.plos.org/plosone/article?id=10.1371/journal.pone.0137260#abstract0. Published 2015. Accessed January 25, 2020.

## THE DANGER OF GOING WITH THE FLOW

When I left my corporate job in 2017, I had not been happy for a couple years. I had been in the same industry for twenty-one years and with the same company for twelve. Though I had been fortunate to have eight different roles over those two decades, in my last job, I found myself in a position for which I hadn't applied, nor was I particularly suited for it from an experience standpoint. I had allowed myself to be painted into a corner.

Sometimes in the corporate world, if you simply go with the flow, you'll find yourself in a place you hadn't intended. I was there and I asked myself,

> *"How did I get here? And what do I want to do about it?"*

Though I was able to do what was required of the job, the energy going out far outweighed the energy coming in, causing me to feel depleted.

## DECIDING TO DIVORCE MY JOB

I had been through ups and downs in my career prior to that time. Ebbs and flows are natural in one's career depending on many factors. I had persevered through times when I wasn't as enamored with my job, only to fall back in love with it. In this situation, that wasn't happening. It was becoming apparent that my job was not a great fit for me anymore.

After a couple years of trying to contort myself to fit into what I thought my role required and being unhappy doing it, I ended up having a frank conversation with my boss about how I wasn't the right fit. After the conversation, I was scared because I realized that I had basically stated my desire for a "divorce" from my job, but strangely enough, my heart sang.

It felt so good to speak my truth. For a long time, I had been waking up on Monday mornings with a feeling of dread that had to be buried to do my job. Obviously, that was not a healthy situation, and it took its toll on me in a number of ways.

## STAYING MAY BE RISKIER THAN LEAVING

Sometimes we just let the days go by unexamined and without intentional action, and then one day we find ourselves in a place we hadn't expected. What do you do at that point?

Only you can answer that question for yourself. There's risk in leaving, but there could actually be more risk in staying. Many professionals have gotten caught unaware by a restructuring or merger and seen their boring but cushy job eliminated.

Even when they weren't happy with their jobs, they were shell-shocked by the prospect of being pushed out. And even worse, many people have retired from a job that they didn't like and looked back and wished they had taken the chance long ago to follow their passion rather than take the safe route.

If you are unhappy or bored with your current career, regardless of the season, what keeps you from exploring a path where you feel vital every day? I encourage you to think about what you get out of your current job and how many of the boxes it ticks for you in terms of job satisfaction.

## USE PRIOR SUCCESS AS A LAUNCHPAD

A block that may keep you from considering a job change is a fear of the unknown. Entertaining worst-case fantasies is natural, but if you have had success in your career in the past, the likelihood of them coming true is low.

If you find yourself considering a change and feeling scared about the future, here's an effective tool that can help you reframe your situation:

**Step 1:** Think of a time when you've been successful.

**Step 2:** Recall the strengths and skills that you used to achieve that goal.

**Step 3:** Decide how you can apply those strengths and skills to your current situation.

## GETTING BACK IN TOUCH WITH YOUR POWER

Often, just the reminder that you've overcome obstacles in the past to achieve goals can be enough to shift to a positive energetic state, preparing you to take action—even a small step—toward your goal. The effort over a long period of time makes the difference—not whether one action works or not.

Sitting around mulling over the perfect next move is just a waste of time.

If you have goals you'd like to reach but are not sure how to make them happen, think back to a time when you were in a similar situation and the outcome was a success. What skills and approaches did you use?

Have courage in knowing that you've faced obstacles and overcome them in the past and you can do it again. You may stumble, but you will also get up and keep moving. That's called progress, and it's not always pretty, but it sure is satisfying when you look back to see how far you've come!

## YOU'RE MORE POWERFUL THAN YOU KNOW

I have a powerful secret to share with you. You are influential, maybe even magical. You're able to create something out of literally nothing. Your thoughts have energy, and some say that you wouldn't imagine a possibility unless it had the potential to become real. Before you write me off as a kook, let me provide a potent example.

When I was a kid back in the 1970s, I read the *Dick Tracy* comic strip in the newspaper. Dick was a police detective with grit, brains, and moxie. One of the things that most intrigued me about Dick Tracy was his "wrist TV" (Which was initially introduced in 1946 as a wrist radio!)[16] He used

---

16   "The Evolution of Dick Tracy's Wristwatch." https://infostory. com/2011/01/24/the-evolution-of-dick-tracys-wristwatch/. Accessed January 25, 2020.

it to summon backup, talk with police headquarters, call for the ambulance, and more.

Long before cell phones, I couldn't imagine this could ever be a possibility outside of the funny pages. Where were the cords? How could they connect? Where did the power come from? So many unanswerable questions! For those of you who have grown up in the digital age, these things puzzled kids back in the pre-internet "old days."

Fast forward to 2020, and we now know that Dick was using the equivalent of the Apple Watch decades before its arrival. In fact, Marty Cooper, the inventor of the first smartphone, attributes Dick Tracy as the inspiration for his revolutionary invention.[17]

Chester Gould, the creator of Dick Tracy, imagined this technology that is so ubiquitous today in a time when many people didn't have radios in their homes yet, let alone on their wrists.[18] It's likely that Gould had no inkling if this imaginary tool would ever become real, but he put it out into the world and the idea itself ended up inspiring scores of people who had the knowledge and motivation to create the "wrist TV."

---

17  "Video Interview with Marty Cooper." https://sceneworld.org/blog/2015/02/12/video-interview-with-marty-cooper/. Accessed January 25, 2020.

18  O'Connell, Jean Gould. Chester Gould: A Daughter's Biography of the Creator of Dick Tracy. McFarland. 2007. p. 5.

## ENVISIONING YOUR FUTURE

So what's the relevance of this to you and your career? I hope you realize everything that has been accomplished or created started with an idea and intention to make it happen. The same is true of your career. If you're in a situation that is currently not serving you, I want you to know that you have the power to create the situation that you'd like to experience.

Here are the three things that I hope you'll take from this chapter:

- **Have the courage to acknowledge the things you'd like to have in life.** Let your imagination run wild every so often. What do you really want? What would make your heart sing? Now that you have this idea in mind, let yourself really feel what it would be like. What would you do? Where would you go? How would you be? Spend some time writing about it, daydreaming about it, researching it. Let yourself believe in the possibility of this idea without any self-criticism or doubt . . . I mean, what could it hurt to let the idea exist?

- **Be brave and share your idea or wish with others.** Be selective to start with—share with people who are open-minded or who have actually done something similar and see what they think. You may find that as you share your idea, others are excited or inspired by it or at least don't think it's insane. Others may share their ideas or experiences of making their dreams come true, and all this can help to nourish and grow your own idea, and soon you may see paths to it becoming a reality.

- **Seek others who share your aspirations.** If you find the people currently surrounding you are either not supportive or don't understand your vision, look for people who do. Find professional associations in your area of interest and go to a meeting. Join clubs or go to training classes. When you put yourself in the vicinity of others doing things that interest you, you'll learn, see opportunities, and receive support. Don't be afraid to dream. Nothing worthwhile happens without starting with a little seed of an idea. Nurture it and see what grows.

## THE POWER OF CLEAR VISION

I'd like to share a few examples of how a mindset shift toward possibility can be the first step toward changing your reality.

When I was moving across the country for a new job from North Carolina to suburban Chicago, I worried about the expenses—especially housing.

Though I had gotten a big promotion and a raise, it was a stretch to afford a house in a suburb that had everything we wanted. I didn't want to have to sacrifice the amenities of our new home in order to be located near good schools and within walking distance to the train.

With three kids, at least two bathrooms were a necessity, but when we looked at homes in our preferred town in the neighborhoods that were affordable, I found a lot of one-and-a-half bathroom homes or homes that would require driving to the train. Because we would need to sell a car to afford the increased mortgage, proximity to the train was key.

After a whirlwind weekend with a realtor, we found our house. It was slightly more expensive than what we originally wanted to spend, but it had everything . . . same square footage as our old home, walking distance to the train, three full baths, a brand-new kitchen, and an en suite master with a walk-in closet.

We actually got more than we'd originally wanted, but I fully credit my crystal-clear vision about my family's home needs for the successful outcome. I will admit that I had a little fear that we wouldn't find it, but I didn't allow that to shut down my willingness to seek out the perfect house. As St. Matthew wrote, "Seek and you shall find!"

## THE POWER OF A LITTLE FAITH

I have seen similar success with clients who were not happy in their jobs and feared they had no option but to tolerate it. When Frank hired me to help him on his job search, he was in that boat.

Frank had studied accounting in college because his father had advised him it was a stable profession that would provide a good living. He graduated from a top business school and was recruited and hired by a Big Four accounting firm, but after close to ten years in his role, he was bored and feeling stuck in a career that did not align with his creative side. The work was draining him.

When he and I started working together, he had applied for roles at start-ups through online job boards. He felt that the dynamics of a start-up would provide him with more variety and excitement than the big accounting firm where his role was specialized. The reality was that it was a giant and unlikely leap from the Big Four to the start-up world.

Frank and I talked extensively about what he really wanted from his job—what parts of himself did he want to use more in his job? How did he want to feel? What type of culture did he want? Because he had only worked at one company in his professional career, understandably, he didn't know what he didn't know about what opportunities might exist for him in the job market.

## THE POWER OF NETWORKING

I encouraged him to spend less time applying for jobs online and to start reaching out and talking to people in his first- and second-degree network. The intention was to learn what it was like working as an accountant in other types of firms and to share his experience with others who might know about opportunities that would align with his skills, strengths, values, and preferences.

Within a couple months of beginning his networking activities, Frank was introduced to a partner at a regional accounting firm, and they met for coffee. Though the meeting was not an interview, during their conversation, the partner recognized Frank had experience in an area where the firm had a gap. That casual meeting resulted in a job offer, which Frank accepted.

Frank had an appealing new job with a ten-minute commute where he could delve into other areas of accounting that wouldn't have been possible at his old company. He would assume the role of mentor to junior associates and he could take the lead in developing an accounting practice at the firm in his area of specialty. It was a win-win situation that began with Frank's willingness to believe there was a job out there that was a better fit for him, and indeed there was.

## DARE TO DREAM

I'm not suggesting that all you need to do is envision your dream job and it will magically appear. However, if you are not happy in your current role, you will not find a better job unless you give yourself permission to paint a mental picture of what could be.

Give yourself the freedom to imagine your ideal scenario. The worst that could happen is that you don't get it. The reality is that if you don't imagine it, you definitely won't get it, because you won't even recognize the opportunity if it comes your way.

As Norman Vincent Peale[19] said,

> *"Shoot for the moon. Even if you miss,*
> *you'll land among the stars!"*

---

19  Peale, Norman Vincent. https://www.goodreads.com/quotes/4324-shoot-for-the-moon-even-if-you-miss-you-ll-land. Accessed February 1, 2020.

# DEBORAH: REINVENTION AND RESILIENCE AT FIFTY-SIX

———

Despite giving your all to a role, sometimes you may find you are out of a job and feeling poorly treated for reasons outside your control. Not taking it personally can be difficult, and mustering the energy to go out and find a new job can be even more of a burden.

Deborah Day[20] found herself in that situation after decades of dedication to her career and community. She was fifty-five years old without a job and wondering if the foundations she'd always relied on would still be there to support her. Through her faith and resilience, she rose from the depths of despair to find incredible gifts beyond her imagination.

---

20   Name has been changed to protect her privacy.

**IN HER OWN WORDS**

This story ends with me sitting at a bar eating the best caprese salad of my life.

I was brought up in the Deep South. I was the first person in my family to graduate from college, and then I went on to law school. Because my parents had worked so hard to save the money to send me to college, I felt an obligation to make their investment pay off.

### A SOUTHERN "LADY LAWYER"

Mind you, this was the 1970s, a time when it was pretty unusual for women to go to law school. In fact, when I got out of law school and passed the bar, I couldn't find a job in my home state. I went to Florida to practice law because they were more accepting of female lawyers.

### BECOMING A JUDGE

After several years in Florida, my family and I came back home and I started my own law practice. Then, I ran for a judge seat in my county and was elected to a six-year term. In that role, I had the authority to hear criminal cases all the way up to the death penalty, I handled a number of multi-million-dollar civil cases, and I handled domestic cases like divorce, custody, everything.

I had worked in my community all my life. I had volunteered in the schools, was the president of the PTO, and had worked in community theater for more than twenty years.

## THE FUNNY AND THE SERIOUS SIDES OF JUDGESHIP

As a judge, I was well-known in the community. My poor kids, who were teenagers at the time, could not get away with anything. When my daughter got stopped by the local police for a seat belt violation, the officer told her, "Tell your mama I said 'hey.'" They couldn't get away with anything! That was an amusing story, but there were some more serious ones as well.

I had death threats against me. One time I got a message that I needed to look under my car before I "cranked" it, supposedly because a car bomb was attached. That one was investigated and thankfully was nothing more than an idle threat.

Another death threat was related to a custom in my court. Before a trial, I greeted and shook hands with the plaintiffs, defendants, and their families. I got word through an intercepted jailhouse message that the mother of one of the defendants planned to "curse" me with a voodoo potion when I shook her hand. The bailiff who told me was so sweet and really concerned. I wasn't worried, but I didn't want to hurt his feelings.

## RUNNING FOR REELECTION

My judgeship was a really interesting job. My term was ending, and it was time to run for reelection. While I loved the job and enjoyed serving the community, I didn't love the politics. Even though we were well into the twenty-first century, I experienced a clear undertone of misogyny.

Over time and through my persistence, I'd been accepted as a "woman lawyer" in the legal community in my town, but when it really came down to being a judge, many in the community still felt they needed to elect the "best man" for the job. It was a throwback to that old Southern way—a lack of acceptance of women in positions of authority and an attitude that "no woman's going to tell me what to do." It was not pretty.

## A PERSONAL AND POTENT WEAPON

One of my deepest pains during that campaign was when someone got access to the official court system and passed my kids' driving records around town. If they were looking for a weapon, what could be more effective than trying to hurt me by hurting my children? I never found out for certain who did it, but it was painful to realize someone in the community could stoop to that level in an attempt to hurt me.

As a sitting judge, I needed to maintain a stance of neutrality, so it was difficult to defend myself from the implications people were making about me and my family. I endured the mudslinging and hoped for the best in the election.

## OUT OF A JOB AT AGE FIFTY-FIVE

Unfortunately, I lost. I was fifty-five years old and really didn't know what to do next. It seemed extremely unfair. Honestly, I'm not sure what else I could have done to prove myself. I'd done everything I was supposed to do—I followed the rules.

I had a great marriage and wonderful children. I had been active in the schools, in my church, and in the community. Yet that incredible mean-spiritedness was still directed at me and my family. It caused unimaginable personal pain.

The election was in April, but I still had to work through the end of my term in January—a grueling eight months. As painful as it was to consider getting a job in the community, I knew I had to keep working. I had one child in graduate school and another in law school at the time. In addition, I liked working and wanted to do it for my own satisfaction.

### WHAT TO DO NEXT?

After having been impugned during the campaign, I couldn't imagine staying there and practicing law. I felt hurt and wasn't sure who I could trust. That was hard. After what I went through in the campaign, it would have been extremely difficult.

I updated my résumé and started sending it out. I talked to friends over the course of those eight months waiting for the term to end. There I was—still a judge—dealing with people in the community who had inflicted a lot of pain on me and my family and trying to process the anger. That was excruciating.

### AN INTERESTING JOB WITH A LONG TITLE

As I was grappling with what to do next and not really liking the options I saw, one day I noticed a job listing in my church newsletter for an intriguing role with a long title.

They wanted someone with a graduate degree, knowledge of my church's denomination, and experience with women's issues. The parallels with my own background were uncanny. I had been active in my church for decades. I'd been active in employment law and had chaired the sections of the state bar association concerning women's issues and women's rights.

### WAS GOD WRITING MY RÉSUMÉ?

I sat down, looked at this, and said to myself, "Okay, I'm a person of faith. I'm going to own this." It was like God had been writing my résumé specifically for this job, because everything in the job description was something that I had done, from the law degree to being on the church committee. I had to deal with a division of sexual misconduct to be elected to the state bar leadership positions.

The job seemed perfect for me, with one small issue—the job was located in Chicago. I mean, I wasn't thirty-five. I was going on fifty-six years old. I grew up in the deep South. I did not own a winter coat. It was a quandary—what to do! I talked to my husband, my kids, and good friends. The answer from everyone was to apply.

### MY FIRST WINTER COAT

In the middle of January, a week after my fifty-sixth birthday, wearing the puffy Michelin Man coat my husband had thoughtfully given me for Christmas, I got off a plane at Midway International Airport for my first visit to Chicago. I rode the orange line from the airport, got off in the middle of the Loop, and walked to the office for my interview.

I was a little old for so many "first time ever" experiences, yet here I was—first time in Chicago, first time taking public transportation, first time walking the city streets alone at night. I made it to my interview, and I got the job!

In case you're wondering about my living arrangements, I worked it out that I would split my time between my home and Chicago, flying up for a week or two each month. During my first week on the job, I stayed at a Hampton Inn and, for dinner each night, grabbed soup or a sandwich on the way back to the hotel. But on Thursday night before I was to fly home, I decided to treat myself to a solo celebration dinner at an Italian restaurant in the middle of the Chicago Loop.

### VICTORY IS SWEET

I sat at the bar and ordered a caprese salad and glass of red wine and toasted myself that at age fifty-six, somehow, I had found the courage to completely change careers, and do all of these things for the first time.

Only a few months before, my family and I had been enduring the pain of that horrible election—all the mean things written in the papers, all the untrue radio ads. And here I was in a new city, starting a new chapter, eating the best darn salad of my life. Resilience is sweet.

**EXERCISE: DEVELOPING RESILIENCE**

Write out answers to these questions to help you discover your own well of resilience:

- When have you been severely disappointed? What did you do to recover?
- What resources do you have that you can tap into if you lose your job? Savings? Network? Credentials?
- If you realize that your existing resources are not adequate to support you in the event of a job loss, what can you do now to prepare?
- How clear are you on your strengths and how you add value to organizations you've worked for?
- How clearly and concisely can you communicate the value you provide in the workplace?
- How well established is your self-care routine? Is it currently serving you well or do you need to develop new habits?
- How much sleep are you getting?
- Are you refraining from excessive self-medicating behaviors with alcohol and other substances?
- Are you making time to enjoy family and friends?
- Are you eating and hydrating to maintain your health?

- Who can support you from a mental and emotional standpoint?

If you feel depressed, anxious, or confused, consider getting support from a friend, therapist, coach, religious counselor, or going through your company's employee assistance program.

When you have taken an inventory of your available resources and have developed a contingency plan for potential career detours, you can rest easier knowing you will be able to deal with whatever difficulties come your way.

## CHAPTER 5

# WHEN YOU'RE DEALT A BAD HAND: Coping With Toxic Work Situations

---

*God, grant me the serenity to accept the things*
*I cannot change, courage to change the things*
*I can, and wisdom to know the difference.*

—REINHOLD NIEBUHR[21]

## TOXIC WORKPLACES ARE COMMON

Workplaces can become toxic when the work demands, culture, and/or coworkers cause serious disruptions in the rest

---

21  Shapiro, Fred R. "Who Wrote the Serenity Prayer?" The Chronicle of Higher Education. https://www.chronicle.com/article/Who-Wrote-the-Serenity-Prayer-/146159/ April 28, 2014. Accessed January 25, 2020.

of your life.[22]  According to a 2019 research report published by the Society of Human Resource Management (SHRM), nearly two-thirds of working Americans have worked in a toxic work environment at some point in their career, and twenty-six percent have worked in more than one.[23]  That's truly astounding!

We spend a lot of time working, and most of us are dependent on work for income and a sense of purpose. When work becomes toxic, it can have a devastating impact on both job and life satisfaction.

Here's a story of a toxic work environment that I lived through back in the late 1990s and the lessons I came away with.


## IN COMES SHELLY THE SCREAMER

About four years into an otherwise great job, I had my first encounter with workplace toxicity. My department was restructured and the department leader who worked in another city hired a new director for our office. Shelly left a global consulting firm for this role and moved to the Southern city where the company was headquartered.

---

22  Housman, Michael and Minor Dylan. "Toxic Workers." (PDF) Harvard Business School. Archived from the original (pdf) on 15 August 2019. https://www.hbs.edu/faculty/Publication%20Files/16-057_d45c0b4f-fa19-49de-8f1b-4b12fe054fea.pdf Retrieved 25 August 2019.

23  "The High Cost of a Toxic Workplace Culture" Research Report, SHRM. July 2019. https://www.shrm.org/resourcesandtools/hr-topics/employee-relations/pages/toxic-workplace-culture-report.aspx Accessed January 25, 2020.

Within the department, Shelly made us wary. Her direct style clashed with the gracious and courteous culture of the organization. Admittedly, when I moved there a few years before, I quickly realized that small talk in this culture was a requirement if I wanted to develop productive relationships within the organization. Getting directly down to business, which had been the norm at my employer in DC, was considered rude there.

## CULTURE SHOCK

Shelly was fast moving and direct. And when she became upset, she tended to scream. *(Yes, scream!)* One day, I was unfortunate enough to hear her side of a phone conversation through the office wall I shared with her—at an incredibly high decibel, I heard her berate the dry cleaner in the building for allegedly losing the pants to a suit she'd dropped off for cleaning.

As time went on, I realized this was not a one-time loss of composure on Shelly's part. This type of unhinged behavior became shockingly common. I shook my head and could not believe this was my job and that she was my boss. I mean, who acts like that?

Shelly's approach to management alternated between ingratiation, manipulation, and micromanagement of female subordinates and colleagues. With men, she also included flirtation, which I suppose is a form of manipulation.

Her frequent emotional outbursts tended to be confined to times when only subordinates on the marketing team were present, which meant that it took a while for her dysfunction to become apparent to her business partners, HR, and leadership.

## STRESS AND SELF-MEDICATING BEHAVIORS

I began to dread going to work and encountered health issues such as insomnia, irritability, and anxiety. As much as I hate to admit it, I began drinking wine just about every night after work to relax and forget about the chaotic situation at work. Though I didn't recognize it at the time, I was dealing with a toxic boss in an otherwise supportive workplace.

I was experiencing some of the common responses: depression, anxiety, weight gain, self-medicating behavior, a drop in productivity, and reduced ability to focus. Other common responses include self-harming behaviors, workplace absence, increased illnesses, raised blood pressure, and other negative health effects.

## THE DANGERS OF A TOXIC ENVIRONMENT

A toxic workplace can leave you feeling trapped. Most people work to earn money for material needs and enjoyment. Work can also contribute to self-esteem and a sense of purpose. When you are in a toxic workplace, you can feel like your existence is being threatened, and that can cause you to retreat into survival mode.

You may stop doing the things that you enjoy, which disrupts your ability to relax and recharge. Stress increases, and you may become fixated on how to "solve the problem" of work. In my case, initially, I had a hard time seeing what was really going on as I redoubled my efforts to avoid, then please, my demanding boss.

## COPING WITH A TOXIC WORK SITUATION

Whether or not your bad work situation rises to the level of "toxic" doesn't really matter. If you're finding that work has gone from enjoyable—or at least tolerable—to draining and dreadful, you can take three actions:

1. Do nothing and continue to endure the situation as it is,

2. Leave to find a better situation,

3. Stay and try to improve the current situation—including making changes in your own behavior, discussing the issues with someone who has the authority to effect change, such as HR or a supervisor, or other actions.

To help you decide which path you should take, here are some questions to consider:

### HOW LONG HAS THIS BEEN GOING ON?

Is it related to a specific project or deadline? Can you see the light at the end of the tunnel? If it's a relatively short-term situation, you may want to wait it out. The stressors may pass, and the environment may return to a state that you can tolerate or even go back to enjoying. If this is the "new normal," you may be motivated to make a change.

## WHAT CAUSED THE CHANGE IN THE ENVIRONMENT?

Was it sudden or gradual? Did the situation change due to new leadership or organizational structure, new policies, or a change in market conditions? If you can pinpoint when and where the situation started, you may be able to understand whether you can potentially change or adapt to it.

There's a big difference between lobbying for a change to a poorly-conceived policy and arresting the effects of a tanking economy. Some things you have the power to change, and some you don't. Understanding the root and magnitude of the issues at hand is a good start.

## WHAT INFLUENCE DO YOU HAVE OVER THE SITUATION?

Are those in leadership aware of the impact that the environment is having on you? How able are you to have a frank conversation about it with your boss or another person in a position of influence? Sometimes the issue is not with your boss. It could be coming from higher in the organization and your boss may have little influence on the expectations. Or it could be that your perception of what is expected is not aligned with your boss's.

Getting clarity and bringing ideas to the table on how to do things better is often welcomed. After all, those in leadership may not fully understand the impact their decisions have on your day-to-day experience. Speaking up could result in positive changes. Give it a shot before deciding on more radical actions.

### ARE OTHERS IN YOUR ORGANIZATION HAVING SIMILAR EXPERIENCES? HOW ARE THEY COPING?

Sharing your experiences with coworkers may help you to feel less alone. You could learn tips on how to better "manage up," or build a coalition to influence leaders to make changes. Building alliances with fellow employees can help ensure management doesn't perceive you as a "problem employee" in case a true structural or management problem is at the root of the issue.

### WILL OPPORTUNITIES AT YOUR ORGANIZATION ALLOW YOU TO LEAVE THE TOXIC WORK SITUATION?

Is your boss or department causing the situation, or is it a more systematic malady that exists throughout the entire organization? If the toxicity is confined to your specific department, you may decide to explore other opportunities to leverage your current organizational knowledge and network. If the toxicity is rampant throughout the organization, you may need to get out to save your health and sanity.

### IS THE ENVIRONMENT UNIQUE TO YOUR ORGANIZATION, OR IS IT A REALITY OF THE INDUSTRY?

Can you consult people in your network at other organizations to find out? Your skills and experience may be in demand at another employer that has a better culture or is in a more favorable position in the marketplace. Getting a view of what it's like at other companies can give you information you need to decide if you should stay, go, or try something completely new.

## WHAT DOES IT COST YOU TO REMAIN IN YOUR CURRENT SITUATION? IS YOUR CONFIDENCE WANING?

How is the situation affecting your health and relationships? Sometimes people will stay in a situation for much longer than they should. It's hard to consider leaving without another job, but sometimes it can be the best option before their relationships, health, or confidence are eroded to the point of not having the energy to look for another job.

Sometimes, hanging in there can eventually lead to being fired by an unreasonable manager or pegged as the scapegoat for mistakes. Both of these scenarios can be hard to bounce back from. Though leaving a job without another job is not ideal, sometimes taking control of one's destiny is preferable to continued suffering and abuse.

## HOW EGREGIOUS IS THE SITUATION? HAS IT RISEN TO THE LEVEL OF ILLEGALITY?

Does blatant abuse, harassment, or discrimination take place? Are you able to document it? If the abuse is significant, you may consider consulting an employment attorney to explore your options. Some companies may be open to a negotiated exit, which could include a severance package.

Some employment attorneys provide free consultations, and, even if you need to pay for an hour of their time, it could be well worth the investment. Experienced attorneys often know a lot about specific employers. They may know whether your employer would negotiate or if they've been accused of other employment law violations. At the very least, they can advise you of your rights.

## HOW MUCH OF THIS SITUATION IS BASED IN REALITY AND HOW MUCH IS YOUR PERCEPTION?

Sometimes people will label a situation "toxic" when it's actually just uncomfortable because it requires them to develop new skills, adapt to a new structure, or learn new processes. Take a close look at yourself and ask whether your experience could be different if you responded differently.

If other people are not having issues with the situation, it could be that you need to learn some new skills to cope. It's always helpful to get perspective on the situation. A mentor, coach, or experienced friend can sometimes help you see the bigger picture and help you decide what options you have.

## WHAT'S WITHIN YOUR CONTROL?

Without going into too much detail about my role in the toxic dance with Shelly, suffice to say, initially I didn't handle it well. As a manager, she sought to control me and I, in turn, tried to avoid her. Eventually, I realized that I would hurt myself if I didn't begin to respect her position as my boss.

Because the department leader was in another city, he wasn't witness to her worst behavior, and she was able to control the narrative with him. Any complaints to him from her direct reports were seen as the team getting used to the new structure.

## TAKING CONTROL OF WHAT I COULD

I finally woke up to the fact that I would need to proactively show my support for Shelly even if it meant I had to grit my teeth and paste a smile on my face when I checked in to say hello to her each morning. What I found was that she relaxed and actually began stopping by my office to get my opinion on things.

My job became easier, as I was no longer the target of her vitriol and frustration. Once I turned over this new leaf, I found acceptance of the situation took less energy than the resistant stance I'd previously taken. When I approached the situation differently, Shelly's response to me changed. However, that didn't mean she was reformed.

### SHELLY FINDS A NEW TARGET

Unfortunately, a colleague soon became the new target for Shelly's nitpicking and bullying. Though I knew nothing of it at the time, Shelly's bullying of my coworker was the proverbial "last straw." She had finally overstepped the boundaries between poor management and documented abuse (with witnesses) so that the HR department could take decisive action.

One evening, as I sat in my office finishing up a project, the voicemail light on my phone suddenly blinked red. As the message played, I realized my fervent prayers had been answered. The departmental leader stated that, effective immediately, Shelly was no longer employed by the organization. Shelly's ten-month reign of chaos had ended.

### LASTING LESSONS FROM A HORRIBLE BOSS

As painful as that episode was, I am glad that I went through it. I realize that both despite and because of her poor management skills, I learned several important lessons that have served me well since then:

1. **If you want to lead change, you need to know where you're starting from.** It's important to understand the situation you're entering, communicate a vision, and gain buy-in before trying to lead a change. Shelly had been hired to lead a team that was already high-performing, close-knit, and collegial. She approached the team as if it were in need of a turnaround rather than a basic tune-up, and because she neglected those steps, she met resistance. More open dialogue would have gone a long way to gaining buy-in with the team.

2. **Regardless of the effectiveness (or ineffectiveness) of a supervisor, it's imperative to respect the role.** Avoiding interactions with my boss served no purpose for me or the organization, other than to make me insubordinate. It wasn't my place to pass judgment on her effectiveness. I was also obliged to ask her for what I needed—such as reminding her to provide feedback on the projects she was reviewing so I could keep them on schedule. I needed to be fully responsible for my part of the projects, regardless of whether she was delivering on her side. Though her style was frustrating to me, I had no excuse not to keep up my work commitments or to respect her authority as my manager.

3. **Have a contingency plan.** While it wasn't my place to judge, it would have been wise of me to take note of her lack of effectiveness and document my own actions so I could explain project delays caused by her slow review and approval of project deliverables. If there had been an accounting for why

projects were not being completed on time, the blame could have easily been placed on my shoulders, even though the delay was caused by her failure to provide timely feedback. Though documentation can be time-consuming, sometimes it's a wise insurance policy if you foresee the situation taking a bad turn.

4. **Keep some perspective.** Nothing is forever. During that time, I allowed myself to become highly stressed, and then suddenly, one day, the cause of my stress was gone. At that moment, I realized that I'd been walking around loaded for bear, but suddenly the bear was gone. All at once, those big guns were heavy and unnecessary. At that moment, I realized it had been my choice to be defensive and resentful. In fact, *I* was the cause of my own misery due to my beliefs and how I chose to respond to Shelly.

5. **Working through personnel issues can take some time in the corporate world.** HR issues are confidential and only those who need to know will be privy to what's going on. It may seem like the abusive employee is getting a free pass and that no one in authority is taking notice when, in fact, due process may be moving along behind closed doors. For several months, as Shelly continued to bully and cause mayhem, I believed that the HR department had left me and my coworkers at the mercy of a madwoman. That's what it felt like. I later found out that the department leader was aware of the problem and was working on a resolution with HR.

6. **Beliefs create mind-sets, and we have control over our beliefs.** This is the big takeaway—I was stressed and overwhelmed not because I had an ineffective boss but due to my own beliefs. I was capable of being happy. I could have

chosen to leave work behind when I went home at the end of each day. Instead, I chose to bring the troubles home with me and whine about my situation over a few glasses of wine. When Shelly was gone in a wink, I realized I'd been resisting harder than necessary, and it felt strange when suddenly I had nothing to resist. A huge weight was lifted from my shoulders with that realization!

Working for Shelly wasn't a pleasant time in my life, but I learned some extremely valuable lessons from her, for which I'll be forever grateful. So, to Shelly, wherever you are, thank you for teaching me these lessons. And I hope you found your suit pants.

### IS IT A DEATH SPIRAL OR JUST A BAD DAY?

Sometimes job dissatisfaction is caused by a sudden change like a toxic new boss. At other times, incremental changes may happen over years, and then, one day, you wake up and find yourself in a job you don't like. All you know is that you are not happy and are not sure what to do about it.

It can be hard to distinguish between a series of bad days and the awareness that your job isn't a good fit anymore. At first, you may spend time venting to friends or your significant other, or maybe you go home and crack open the Merlot and have a couple glasses to unwind. Both approaches are fine ways to deal with the stress of an unfulfilling job in the short term. And I stress—short term!

If you notice that your job has changed permanently from the one you used to love to one that overwhelms you with feelings of helplessness and anger, it's time to put a plan in place that will result in longer-term change. Read on for healthy tips on how to make that happen.

1. **Try to figure out if this will pass or if it's not something you can adjust to.** Determine whether the issue with your job is internal or external—or both. Could you get used to the changes with time? For example, maybe the new boss will grow on you as you get to know each other, but if your commute has changed from thirty minutes to two hours due to an office move, it may be harder to get used to. Consider the following questions to make that determination:

- How long has your dissatisfaction been apparent?

- When you first noticed that your feelings for your job were changing, what else was going on? What changed between when you liked your job and now?

- What parts of your job do you still like?

- Have you outgrown your job—do you need a new challenge that this job won't provide?

- If you could change a couple things about your job, would your enthusiasm return?

- Is it you or the job that has changed?

2. **Get some perspective on what's in your control and what's not.** Using the insights you gained from answering the

questions above, brainstorm things that are directly within your control to change or things that you can ask for to make you happier with your job.

- **As you're doing this, refrain from editing yourself.** No "yeah, buts"—as in, "Yeah, but I can't leave this company, I've got kids in college," or "Yeah, but I will never find another job that pays this much in this town," or "Yeah, but it's no better anywhere else." Those types of thoughts will shut down your creative thinking quickly!

- **If something would make you happier if it were changed, ask for it.** Depending on the issues, you might feel happier if you were able to adjust your schedule or the location of your desk or were able to work from home one day a week. Maybe your boss will say no, but maybe they'll say yes. If you don't ask, you don't get.

- **If you're longing for a promotion, have you talked with your boss about what it will take to move ahead?** If you're interested in advancement, make sure your boss knows. Don't expect him or her to read your mind.

3. **Explore your options.** If you've determined your current job is not going to cut it for you anymore, your next step is two-pronged: figure out what will make you happy longer term and determine how to make your current job palatable until you can move on.

- **You may be able to find a new job at your current company.** Check the job postings and reach out to your internal network to learn about potential opportunities. If you don't have a network, start building one. Start by asking a coworker to coffee and build from there.

- **Be sure not to bad-mouth your job, your boss, or the company.** Though you may trust your coworkers, this type of gossip tends to make its way up the hierarchy and could limit both your opportunities within the company and your ability to get a good reference should you decide to go elsewhere. If you need to vent, do it outside of work to people who have no connection to your job.

- **You may feel trapped because you make too much money to leave or don't see a path to a new role.** Some exercises can help you identify your transferable skills and envision how you can combine them in new ways to land a job you'll be happier with. I have included some in this book. *What Color is Your Parachute?* by Richard N. Bolles is also a great source of career self-discovery exercises.

- **Hire a coach.** It can help to have an objective advocate with whom to discuss your situation and help you explore options. As I tell my clients, it's hard to read the label from inside the bottle. You may have skills and strengths that you don't realize are valuable and transferable. If you decide to leave, a career coach can also help you develop a job search strategy so that you can make a smooth transition into a new opportunity that's a good fit.

Options are always available, and you may end up being much better off when you make it to the other side.

## WHAT TO DO IF YOU'RE IN A TOXIC SITUATION

If you are suffering through a toxic, or merely uncomfortable, work situation, you have my profound sympathies. Practice self-care. Get adequate sleep, exercise, eat nutritiously and regularly, hydrate, and make time for enjoyment. Try to take it easy on the booze and other self-medicating substances. If you're not able to manage the stress, seek help.

Many companies have employee assistance programs that will provide some level of support during times of difficulty. Therapy, coaching, and Facebook support groups are all options that can help you cope. Don't suffer alone any longer.

You deserve to enjoy your job and your life!

# PAUL: BUILDING A NEW CAREER ON AN EXISTING FOUNDATION

---

Paul Rudolph[24] is a graduate school instructor teaching on the topic of commercial real estate. He is also a partner in a real estate tech start-up. Paul found his way to teaching and entrepreneurship after spending three decades in investment banking.

Paul's story has been included because, though he has had an unwavering interest in real estate and architecture since boyhood, his career interests related to those topics have evolved over time. After leaving a long-time job, Paul allowed himself to do nothing and get comfortable with discomfort to see what type of guidance he would get. Remaining open

---

24  Name has been changed to protect his privacy.

to opportunities has enabled him to renew his excitement about real estate and discover some new interests as well.

When you're clear on what you're good at and what you like, as Paul has been, you have a clear lens through which to view opportunities when they present themselves so you know if they might be something you'd be happy doing.

## IN HIS OWN WORDS

I grew up in New York City at a time when it wasn't necessarily a nice place to be. It wasn't where all the young people wanted to live, work, and play—that concept had not yet been created. At the time, the urban environment was somewhat challenging.

### AN EYE FOR ARCHITECTURE

As a child, it always fascinated me to see how different communities coped with life within the urban environment. I also had an interest in buildings. I appreciated the different designs and architectural styles. Although some members of my family are involved in the arts, growing up, I would say my calling was more in the financial and mathematical arena. When I was young, I didn't know that career options like architects or urban planners even existed. I was definitely more quantitatively focused, as opposed to focusing on the fine arts.

### A QUANTITATIVE PATH WITHIN LIBERAL ARTS

I graduated first in my class in high school and got into Dartmouth, which is a strong liberal arts university. When

I was in college, I considered majoring in psychology. I was fascinated by the human mind and why we do what we do. I enjoyed economics as a way to explain how the world works, but the class that really changed my direction was Introduction to Statistics.

The professor was a true academic luminary who had been a student of Albert Einstein. He taught my introductory statistics class, and the perspective he shared really hit home. He provided a lens through which to view the world in a way that had a huge impact on me.

Because my dad financed my education, he had some influence on my choice of majors and urged me to get a degree that would be relevant and in demand in the job market. I ended up majoring in economics and statistics.

## THE RULES ARE DIFFERENT AT WORK

When I was in high school, I got top grades and was good at standardized testing. I knew the rules of the game and how to play, so I was successful in an academic environment. When I graduated from college, I thought I could easily figure out the rules in the workplace and be successful. I felt that the rules would be directly transferable. That was far from the reality.

A big eye-opener for me was seeing peers who had been in the middle of the class having career success that was exceptional. That caused me to reevaluate and ask, "Well, what did they bring to the workforce that I wasn't bringing? Why did they get the job? Why were they succeeding in the job despite not having the best academic credentials?"

### EMBARKING ON A CAREER IN FINANCE

After college, I went to work for a big financial services firm. Luckily for me, as I was getting established at the firm, the real estate sector was heating up. Eventually an opportunity opened up that allowed me to combine my childhood interest in real estate with my fledgling finance career. I was happy living out my childhood dream.

Early in my career, I was laid off . . . twice. And I took it personally. In retrospect, I recognize it had nothing to do with me—I was laid off as part of a group or other factors caused the layoff. That's just the way the industry worked, and I just needed to learn how to accept that. If I was going to work at a large international firm, I needed to be prepared for the fact that my job was always tenuous.

### A GOOD CAREER FOR THE EASILY DISTRACTED

I got a job as an investment analyst where I was charged with analyzing the strategies and operations of companies so I could make investment recommendations. I have a short attention span, meaning I like to do a lot of smaller and different tasks rather than one large, routine task. I don't know if that's good or bad, but I recognized that, and luckily, I chose a profession that allowed for a good match between my need for variety and the needs of the job.

I was fortunate that it turned out that way, because I didn't consciously look at a job description and say, "I'm gonna love doing that." Instead, I'd say, "Yeah, I'm capable of doing that." Whether I'd love it wasn't a consideration, just a happy by-product. I feel like so much of what I learned in my career was happily accidental. I didn't catch on to the concept of aligning what I like to do with what the company valued until recently.

Eventually, I pursued a full-time graduate degree in real estate development at MIT. It was perfect, aligning my interests with the academic study of real estate. I've had really a wonderful thirty-plus-year career working for large international financial services companies focused specifically on real estate—different firms but always the same functional occupation.

## DEVELOPING NEW SKILLS TO SUCCEED

After leaving college, I recognized a whole bunch of attributes besides academic skills were highly valued in the workplace. Certain areas in the marketplace highly valued academic skills and people with the best grades, like academic scholars and those pursuing a PhD, but these weren't the opportunities that interested me.

Early in my career, I was confident in my ability to perform the requirements of the jobs I held. It was my lack of interpersonal skills that made me nervous. I wasn't a good public speaker and would get nervous in interview situations. That's where I needed improvement if I wanted to succeed at work.

Since then, I've pursued a lifelong process of improving my public speaking skills. Even though I've done a lot of public speaking at this point, I still consider myself a little dorky and not necessarily the best presenter. I've had to learn by necessity to get better at it and to practice and pay attention to the areas where I need improvement.

## FAKE IT UNTIL YOU MAKE IT

In my first big job out of graduate school, I had a high-profile spot at the firm. In a daily morning call, the investment analysts, of which I was one, would be asked to speak for two minutes about their stock investment ideas. The best analysts would speak clearly and concisely off the cuff with few notes. They were incredibly skilled at making a convincing argument with seemingly little preparation. I could not do that, yet I still had to present my recommendations.

I would prepare a script with every single word typed out, and I would read it word for word. With people in the room and on the phone, I couldn't sound like I was reading it. So I had to practice it five or ten times, going through it, making sure my voice was confident and I had the right intonation to express the enthusiasm that I felt about the recommendations. That worked really well for me and was the crutch I needed to get to the next level.

The people in the room saw that I was reading my recommendations, but ultimately, they didn't care. It didn't impact the quality of the recommendations I was making. Hopefully, I sounded just like the other analysts who were speaking off the cuff. Of course, years later, I became that person who could speak without notes, because by that point, I had all the tools in my head and knew what I wanted to say. I just had to go through my own process to get there.

### REINVENTION GETS TIRING

I spent the last twelve years of my career in investment banking at an employee-friendly company. I was comfortable there for many years. Eventually, all the people around me changed, not once, not twice, but three times in a matter of a couple years.

Although I had the same role for twelve years, it was essentially like I was starting out brand-new at three different companies because all the people I worked with on a day-to-day basis turned over. It became exhausting to always be the "new employee" in this company I'd worked in for so many years.

I adapted to the changes that each successive leader wanted me to make. I reinvented myself but, after a while, it was not much fun. When I was asked to reinvent myself a second and third time, it became frustrating. That's how I finally came to the conclusion that after twelve years, it might be time for me to think about doing something else.

The lack of a consistent strategy or clarity of focus got old. I'm in my fifties, and I briefly considered trying to hang in there for another three years so I could reach my financial goals, but I decided I just couldn't hold on that long. I wasn't enjoying it, and I didn't want to just hang on.

### THE FUTURE WAS UNCLEAR

When I left, I planned to use the time to travel, assess, and evaluate what I wanted to do next. I had no expectations on the day I left for what I would do even the next day. I allowed myself some time to process and think about it.

After a few months, I got to a darker place. It hit me like a lightning bolt that I wasn't associated with any big franchise as I had been for decades. I had no offers coming in that were any different than what I had been doing. I wasn't really looking, and I'm not sure what type of job would have been exciting to me anyway. I didn't do anything, and nothing happened.

I was okay for a few months, but then self-doubt emerged. I saw other people leave and do different things, going from high-functioning Wall Street jobs to opening up a craft distillery or things like that. I didn't have another passion that I immediately knew I wanted to jump into.

I wanted to do more vacation-type things like travel or volunteer overseas. I was at a disadvantage because I didn't know what I wanted to do from a job standpoint. Nothing was grabbing me.

### A NEW CAREER IN TEACHING

I knew professors at the NYU Graduate School of Real Estate just from being in the industry—they were professional colleagues. One day, I got a call about a week before the fall semester started and was asked to teach a class because an instructor had dropped out last minute. I agreed to do it.

I started teaching. It was a lot more work and a lot more fun than I thought it would be. I updated my LinkedIn profile with the position at NYU, then a woman from South Africa called me about helping develop an online real estate class for none other than my alma mater, MIT.

## THE START-UP GAME AS A FIFTY-SOMETHING

I'm now working on a real estate tech start-up idea with a former colleague who I worked with at Merrill Lynch twenty-five years ago. It's been fascinating, intellectually stimulating, and very rewarding to be involved in this. At first, I was a little bit intimidated to think that I would be in the tech industry.

I thought I was too old to have the skills for it. But being old can be an advantage. The skills I have—experience in real estate with connections and an understanding of the industry—are the skills they needed. It's a good fit.

## A NEW PROFESSIONAL FOCUS

One of the great activities I've gotten a lot of energy from is mentoring students at MIT and Fordham. It's been really fun and rewarding. You know that old saying about learning more from my students than they learn from me? That's totally true. That's exactly the way I feel, because the students are super-qualified, so they get everything I teach them.

At first, I was concerned that volunteering could be a time drain, but it hasn't been like that at all. It has been a wonderful, unexpected benefit to me. Since I've been out of school for so long, one of the great advantages of mentoring students at MIT is that it has helped me to be more connected to the school and understand what it's like on campus these days. I understand the campus a lot better and I feel more welcome there. Working there has also been a huge benefit as I work with this real estate start-up, which is not inconsequential to me.

It's been great. I haven't found a destination yet, but I've definitely found a path. And that's really fun.

**EXERCISE: SAYING YES TO OPPORTUNITY**

Spend some time thinking about and writing out answers to the following questions:

- What networks can you tap for opportunities?
  - Alumni groups
  - Professional associations
  - Current and former employer networks
  - Friends and neighbors
  - Networking groups
- What types of job opportunities are at the intersection of your interests, experience, and market opportunities?
- What need does the marketplace have that you can and want to fill?
- If you were to package your skills and experience in a different way, what other opportunities might open up for you?
- If you're interested in doing something different, have you let people know?
- How complete and updated is your LinkedIn profile?
- Does your profile include a professional headshot?
- Do you list and describe all your relevant roles on your profile?

- If you're looking for a job, does your LinkedIn headline include the title of the job you're looking for?
- Are you connected to at least five-hundred people on LinkedIn? If not, look for people who share connections with you through your alma mater, employers, industries, or functional roles and send out connection requests to them.
- Are you remaining open to opportunities? Have you rejected offers, discussions, or other outreach without fully exploring them? Sometimes opportunities come dressed differently than we expect. It never hurts to have a conversation.

## CHAPTER 6

# GETTING YOUR HEAD IN THE GAME: Myths and Lies That Keep You Stuck

———

*We do not see the world as it is, we see it as we are.*

—ANAÏS NIN[25]

My friend Joan and I had just walked out of a quaint French bistro. My meal was delicious, the wine was chilled and refreshing, the conversation was stimulating, and the service was adequate. To me, it had been an enjoyable evening catching up with an old friend. It soon became evident that Joan did not feel the same way.

———

25    Nin, Anaïs. *Seduction of the Minotaur.* The Swallow Press, 1961. p. 124.

As we walked to the car, she railed about the terrible service our waiter had provided and insisted on going over every breach of wait service protocol. Clearly, Joan and I had different expectations of what constituted a successful dinner.

## THE POWER OF PERSPECTIVE

You've undoubtedly experienced something similar when you and a friend, spouse, or colleague witnessed what seemed to be the same situation, only to come away with radically different judgments about what happened. Perhaps you've wondered how that could be.

The simple answer is that you and your companion perceived the situation differently because you had different beliefs and expectations. Based on your life experiences, you have developed your own perspective.

"And why is that?" you may ask . . . and again, the simple answer is that you and your companion have lived two different lives. You've each been on your own journeys and have been taught different values by the people in your lives—parents, teachers, friends, and other influencers. Based on your own life experiences, you each developed your own unique perspectives—the lenses through which you see the world.

## THERE'S NO OBJECTIVE REALITY

You may find yourself in conflict with others because you don't recognize your perception is different than theirs. You may believe others see the world the exact same way that you do and are simply choosing to do something wrong or offensive or against the rules.

However, even people close to you don't believe the exact same things you do. Because of their different experiences, they may not subscribe to your rules and, in fact, their rules may be the exact opposite of yours—for reasons that make total sense to them.

There's no objective good or bad or right or wrong in life, despite what you may have been told growing up. As you go through life, you develop coping mechanisms to deal with your experiences, and through these experiences, you create rules based on the environment in which you were raised. These rules helped you navigate your world successfully.

For example, if your parents expected you to ask to be excused from the table, you did it or risked disapproval. It may seem rude to you to witness someone not using good manners when they abruptly leave the table. You may judge them harshly because they are violating what to you is a rule, but they may have grown up in a less-structured household where it wasn't expected. Based on their upbringing, they may view that request to be silly and unnecessary.

## WHAT'S IN YOUR BAG?

As each of us goes through life, we pick up these rules and expectations and throw them in a metaphorical bag that we carry with us everywhere we go. We carry this bag of beliefs because we believe it will help us to be successful and cope with situations that may arise based on our experiences up to that point.

The bag can get a little heavy at times, especially when we have rules that contradict each other or are outdated. Here's an example of rules that could contradict each other: "Listen to your mother" and "Think for yourself." Here's an example of a rule that may have served you well as a child but not as an adult: "Be seen and not heard."

You are probably aware of some rules you adhere to and you can recognize them through comments like, "That's just the way I was raised," or "Our family has always done it that way." Other rules you learned at such a young age or so consistently that you don't even realize you're following them and therefore never question them. They are like the air you breathe—you don't think about them. They are essentially invisible to you.

These rules could be something like, "Mother knows best," or "Listen to brother because he's the smart one." These invisible rules can sometimes trip you up because you may follow them blindly, even to the point that they begin to hurt you.

### TRIPPING OVER HIDDEN OBSTACLES
When you're unaware of what's in your bag, it can be confusing. You may chronically trip over the same self-imposed stumbling block and with true anguish ask yourself, "Why does this always happen to me?"

Usually, when you have a repeating pattern in your life, it's because of a subconscious belief that you are following. You can experience pain when a subconscious belief contradicts a conscious desire. This conflict can show up as self-sabotaging behavior—when you say you want one thing and yet behave in a way that ruins your progress. This internal and unseen conflict between competing beliefs can cause a lot of pain and frustration until the beliefs are made conscious and resolved.

When these rules are violated or your expectations aren't met, it's naturally upsetting—but you may not even realize why you feel as you do! You may say to yourself, "These are the rules, and someone is not living up to them!" The reality is that the stuff in your bag is creating the lens through which you view your life and experiences. Because we each have different lenses, we're each going to see the world differently, and that may lead to conflict or pain.

### WHAT MIGHT BE IN JOAN'S BAG?

Let's revisit my dinner with Joan. I eat out frequently and viewed the dinner as a great opportunity to spend time catching up with a friend. I was more focused on our conversation than the meal. I had empathy for our waiter because I had been a waitress in college. I chalked up his awkwardness to being new.

With three youngsters at home, Joan was looking forward to treating herself to an "adults only" meal at a nice restaurant. In addition, she was a bit of a connoisseur and was put off by the waiter's lack of knowledge and fumbling wine service. To her, the rookie mistakes were inexcusable and didn't align with her expectations for dinner at an upscale bistro.

### BELIEFS ABOUT WORK

Often, a similar dynamic happens in the workplace. You may have certain expectations about how quickly you'll advance in your career, what projects you'll work on, or the type of recognition and rewards you'll receive.

Your beliefs may be formed by any number of factors—your compensation in relation to that of friends or peers, how quickly someone else advanced in his or her career, what your school advisor told you to expect, what you've read in articles or books, or your own self-perception, among other things.

When your expectations are not met, it can be disappointing—it can even sap your motivation and enthusiasm for the job, moving you further from your goal of career success. When this happens, don't give in to the temptation to feel sorry for yourself.

## REALIGNING EXPECTATIONS

When you're working hard and not getting the results you desire, a misalignment between your expectations and what's required in the job may be at fault. To set yourself up for advancement, talk with your boss to clarify the expectations for your role and ask for regular feedback on where you're meeting those expectations and where you're not. If you are falling short, remain humble, believe in yourself, and ask for the support you need to succeed.

If you find yourself getting emotional about things and you're not sure why, open your bag to see what assumptions, beliefs, and self-sabotaging messages you may be carrying around with you. It may be time to clean out the bag to see the world through a clearer lens. Reexamine your beliefs to understand if they are still serving you and replace outdated beliefs with new ones that serve you better. By becoming fully responsible for your experience in the world and at work, you will find you always have choices and will feel calmer and more in control of your experience.

## BUSTING MYTHS THAT KEEP YOU STUCK

Many successful but unsatisfied professionals work hard and follow the rules they believe will lead to advancement only to be disappointed and wonder what they did wrong when their expectations aren't met. A few myths common among high achievers keep them from leveraging their full potential for professional success.

Oftentimes, the rules they followed in school or at the junior levels of their careers worked well at one time but no longer yield the results they expect as they progress. Let's bust these myths so you can create more effective strategies to find the success you desire.

### MYTH #1:
### RELENTLESS FOCUS ON WORK WILL PUT YOU ON THE FAST TRACK TO PROMOTION.

Leon works hard from nine to five and sometimes even seven to seven with few breaks and no chitchat so he can get his work done. He avoids hanging out in the break room or going to lunch with his coworkers because . . . duh, work! When the team convenes at the local tavern for happy hour, he declines because he wants to get a head start on the projects due the following week. For Leon, work is work and personal is personal, and never the twain shall meet. He figures that's okay, because he knows his boss appreciates his dedication and feels confident he'll be recognized when raise and promotion time comes.

### MYTH #1 BUSTED:
### WORKING HARD DOES *NOT* GUARANTEE YOU'LL GET AHEAD.

Leon is overlooking an important fact: what matters in the workplace is impact—not how many hours he puts in. If you've found yourself focused more on your effort and less on outcomes at work, here are some questions to consider:

- Are you working on the high-priority projects or are you working on the tasks you're most comfortable with?
- Are you bringing fresh ideas to the table?
- Are you solving problems that enable productivity and profitability?
- Are your priorities aligned with those of your boss?

Being the workhorse of a department can cause you to be stuck in your current role. If you are doing work that no one else wants to do and you're seemingly happy to do it, your boss may keep you in that position and promote others over you. And part of the reason could have something to do with those lunches and happy hours your coworkers took time to attend when you didn't.

People like to work with people they know, like, and trust. As employees move up in organizations, relationships become even more important, and those who spend time cultivating a network will be more effective at getting things done.

## MYTH #2:
## YOUR WORK WILL SPEAK FOR ITSELF.

Beth is smart and hardworking, and she's confident that everyone around her recognizes that. She prides herself on being concise and to the point with her updates in the staff meetings. She's not like those tiresome colleagues who drone on about all the stuff they are doing in minute detail every week. Beth prefers to let her work speak for itself. She knows her boss notices that she works harder and produces so much more than those coworkers who brag about all their accomplishments. Beth knows that, when review time comes, she'll get good marks because she works *hard*—certainly her boss and everyone can see that!

## MYTH #2 BUSTED:
## YOU CAN'T ASSUME YOUR BOSS KNOWS WHAT YOU ARE DOING.

This myth is closely related to Myth #1, and if Beth continues to adhere to it, chances are she'll be disappointed. Beth's boss supervises a team of people, has work of her own, and also has to meet the expectations of her own boss. In other words, Beth's boss is busy and distracted.

Don't make the same mistake Beth is making. If you want your great work to be recognized, you've got to let your boss know on a regular basis. The workplace is not like school—people in the same department are often working on different things, and unless you're in sales, there's usually no way to objectively measure and compare the value that each employee contributes. Those who work hard and aren't shy about tooting their own horn usually do better at review time than those who take the silent-but-hopeful approach to letting their work speak for itself.

To ensure you get credit for your results, it's critical to provide regular updates to your boss either monthly or bi-weekly in one-on-one or staff meetings. If neither of those is possible, send your boss a periodic email update documenting completed and in-process projects.

If you get praise from others within the organization for results you've achieved, ask them to put the feedback in an email to you with a cc: to your boss. Rightly or wrongly, often it's what others say about you that has the most impact on how you're viewed and valued within an organization. Make sure everyone knows what you've accomplished so when they do mention you, what they say is accurate.

## MYTH #3:
### THE BOSS'S OPINION IS THE ONLY ONE YOU NEED TO HEED.

Emily's boss loves her because her projects are flawless, completed on time, and under budget. She's dedicated to the mission of her department and obsessively focuses on and prioritizes her team's goals over requests from other areas of the company. After all, why should she allow those requests to distract her from her own department's goals? In Emily's mind, efficiency is the name of the game, and requests for help from other departments are a distraction from the important work of achieving her immediate team's goals.

**MYTH #3 BUSTED:**
**ADVANCEMENT DECISIONS MAY**
**REQUIRE AGREEMENT FROM A COMMITTEE.**

Emily shouldn't count on her laser-focused dedication being rewarded at review time. At many organizations, checks and balances ensure consistent and equitable standards for performance ratings and promotions across the firm.

It's common for committees to review and have veto power over requests for above-average ratings and promotions. Emily's boss will probably need to make the case for her promotion to others, and if Emily has been branded as "not a team player" within the greater organization, it may hurt her chances of promotion.

Your boss's word alone may not be enough to make it through the committee if no one else knows you or is familiar with your achievements. Make a conscious effort to build a positive reputation outside of your department so that others can speak for the quality of your contributions and character. Looking at the big picture and being collaborative could earn you the goodwill required to win a promotion, raise, or larger bonus.

Not being known outside your department or being loyal only to your boss can also be dangerous, especially if your boss were to move on. Without a broader network of people who know the quality of your work and reputation, you may not have the broad-based support to maintain your stature within the company.

## THREE GUIDING TRUTHS

There you have it. To get ahead and have more fun at work, replace these three myths with these three guiding truths:

1. **Work hard and have fun with your coworkers.** Relationships are important because people like to work with people they know, like, and trust. Let yourself be known. Build relationships so you receive the flow of information, so others will want to help you, and so they can provide honest feedback on the value you contribute.

2. **If you're doing great work, tell people.** Ask your boss how they'd like to be kept informed of your accomplishments. If other people give you positive feedback, ask them to document it and share it with your boss. Share your expertise with others, and you'll probably find others are willing to do the same for you. It creates win-win situations where you both grow and the organization becomes stronger overall.

3. **Balance your team's work with helping coworkers within the broader organization.** Through collaboration and a positive attitude, you'll cultivate fans within your broader organization so that when leaders ask who the rock stars are, the answer will be *you*!

## FIVE BIG LIES THAT CAN HOLD YOU BACK

As an executive coach, I often speak with people who have big dreams and want to pursue them but haven't started yet. They come to me in hope of finding support, because they find it hard to know how to get started on their own. They may feel frustrated and stuck and aren't sure what to do about it.

What I've found is that, deep down, they know exactly who they are and what will make them happy, but, for some reason, they are afraid to give in to their desires. I try to help them peel back the layers and uncover and reframe the fears so they don't seem so insurmountable.

Five common excuses prevent people from pursuing paths that will make them happier. Maybe you've encountered one or more of these five big lies. If you're tired of being held back from what you'd like to experience in your life and work, let's break these lies down so you can more easily conquer them:

### BIG LIE #1: I HAVE TO TAKE A BIG LEAP.

It's natural to feel like making a change in your life is a big, scary leap, but you are the one who decides how big a leap it is—or if it's a leap at all. When I started my business, I was frozen at times because I told myself I had to take the plunge like an Acapulco cliff diver.

A wise friend pointed out that I could start in the baby end of the pool if I wanted to. That mental reframing helped me make progress at a pace I was comfortable with and allowed me to gain confidence without causing panic. Before I knew it, like a kid learning to swim, I was jumping into the deep end with energy and joy. Had I held on to the original big lie that a swan dive off a craggy cliff was the only way to get started, I'd still be huddled under the covers biting my fingernails to the quick.

### THE STRAIGHT DOPE

Take a small action in the direction of your goal. As the adage goes, "A trip of a thousand miles starts with a single step." What's one little baby step you can take today?

## BIG LIE #2: I'M NOT READY.

The interesting thing about this statement is that no one ever says it unless there's some expectation of action. If you expect something, part of you wants it. When you say you aren't ready, that's your fear talking.

To address this in a positive way, ask yourself, "What's the smallest action I can take that is impossible to fail at?" Much like Big Lie #1, you are one-hundred percent in control of the action you decide to take and when you decide to take it. It can be as small as deciding that yes, you are ready to take one small action. Once you have even a little momentum, the next step becomes that much easier.

### THE STRAIGHT DOPE

Your first step could be as simple as doing a Google search, making a phone call, or having a conversation with someone who can provide some insights. Those are legitimate steps toward your goal. And if you find yourself hesitating, use Mel Robbins's five second rule. Count down. "Five, four, three, two, one . . . go!" Then act. This technique helps you get started before your consciousness can resist. She has a great TED talk on this technique, which is worth watching.

### BIG LIE #3: THIS DECISION IS DO-OR-DIE.

This can be a showstopper. Perhaps you don't act because you think the result must be perfect or the impact must be huge. This is like a baseball player coming to the plate and expecting to hit a home run every time. An expectation like that leads to performance anxiety and can decrease the likelihood of anything productive happening.

If you detach yourself from the outcome and focus instead on taking action, you can try something different each time until you figure out what works. This approach can even be fun—you may find yourself approaching your tasks with curiosity wondering what will happen next.

**THE STRAIGHT DOPE**

Try stuff . . . and be kind to yourself. Give yourself credit for being brave and notice what parts work and what you want to change next time. Keep up your activity and, before you know it, you'll be getting on base and maybe even hitting the occasional home run. Consistent, small steps will get you closer to your goal than expecting dramatic surges forward.

**BIG LIE #4: NOBODY WILL TAKE ME SERIOUSLY.**

Often, when we decide to do something different, we fear others won't take us seriously. When you have these thoughts, remember that confidence is contagious. When you have confidence in yourself, others tend to have confidence in you as well. If you doubt yourself, others pick up on that and doubt you.

Occasionally, you may encounter someone who rains all over your parade, but that's about them. Your boldness may trigger envy or fear in others that they project onto you so they don't have to deal with their own emotions. When you decide to make a change, do your best to be around supportive, like-minded people who bolster you rather than undermine you.

## THE STRAIGHT DOPE

A saying I know is relevant to this situation: "What other people think of you is none of your business." Focus on what *you* want and what *you* need to do to make it happen. Support yourself in the same way you'd support a friend or loved one who was trying something new and scary.

And if things don't go according to plan, recognize it's all part of the journey. You've learned a lesson that will make you more effective in the future. Give yourself some grace and keep moving forward

> *"What other people think of you is none of your business."*

## BIG LIE #5: PEOPLE WHO ARE SUCCESSFUL ARE DIFFERENT THAN ME.

Pardon my bluntness, but I'm just going to call this one what it is—a self-serving excuse. The only difference between you and someone who is successfully doing what you'd like to do is that they took a chance and did it.

It's easy to sit back and dream and never take action. We have many reasons we tell ourselves not to follow our dreams, but imagining someone else was successful because they had it easier is not valid or relevant.

## THE STRAIGHT DOPE

Someone else's success has nothing to do with you and vice versa. They put their foot on the path and started walking in the direction of their goal. They figured it out step by step . . . and you can too! Don't compare yourself to others. Your journey is your journey and no one else's. Whatever it is that you want to do, just get started.

## THE TRUTH ABOUT THESE FIVE BIG LIES

These lies can seem like ferocious tigers standing between you and your dreams. Maybe you're not pursuing your goals because they seem threatening, but when you have the courage to look more closely, you see they are actually paper tigers that can be conquered with a breath or a flick of the finger.

Remember:

- **You're in control of how big of a risk you take.** Lots of small steps can often get you to your destination faster than a single giant leap.

- **Explore the block that is keeping you from taking even the smallest action.** If you want to do something but feel that you're not ready, you may need to start walking on the path toward your goal to see your options.

- **Few decisions are do-or-die.** Through mistakes, we learn the most and gain the most valuable insights about our true path. Try to reframe mistakes as learning opportunities.

- **Other people's judgment is more about them than it is about you.** Judgment by others never feels good, but the more you recognize that truth, the less it will matter to you. You're responsible for yourself, not for other people's reactions to you and what you decide to do with your life. Be free!

- **People who become successful aren't magical or preordained.** They had an idea of what they wanted, and they took action to bring that idea to life. You have the same power. Be brave and start believing. The more you use your power, the stronger it gets, and the more you'll believe in yourself!

## SHINE THE LIGHT OF TRUTH

Next time you see something that you really want to do and you're second-guessing yourself, stop to see if one of these five big lies is the culprit. Use these tricks to shine the light of truth on what's really going on and move bravely to seize what you really want out of your life.

# ANDREW, PART 1: THE STORYTELLER'S ORIGIN STORY

---

Andrew Linderman is the founder and head storyteller of The Story Source in New York. Though he comes from a long line of entrepreneurs, he gave it a shot in the corporate world as an economist before he recognized he could not escape his family legacy. From that point forward, he followed his passion for theater, improv, and storytelling and created his company in an almost organic way.

Andrew's story is one of deep lows and towering highs. Throughout his career, he has been driven to perfect his craft and share his passion for storytelling because he believes it helps people live more authentic lives. Though Andrew has enjoyed sudden and impressive material success as well as some shocking disappointments, he has remained steadfast in his knowledge that showing up authentically in his life is worth more than anything.

What I hope you will glean from his story is that the sweetness of being true to yourself is a worthwhile pursuit, and that, even in the face of failure and disappointment, resurrection is always possible.

## IN HIS OWN WORDS

I run a company called The Story Source that helps people incorporate personal narratives into their lives and work with the overall goal of creating opportunities. I work with mid-career and senior professionals in a variety of industries and functional areas and help them leverage their personal stories to gain buy-in in their professional lives. Often, their jobs require them to pitch, make presentations, and influence.

I also provide training on public speaking and the art of effective conversation, which is a critical skill in personal and professional contexts. I focus a lot on networking, which makes a lot of people nervous. When people develop effective skills in these areas, it can be transformative.

### THE STORYTELLER'S ORIGIN STORY

I studied a variety of things in college. First, philosophy, then environmental economics. Then, I ended up taking an English class at UC Berkeley that opened my eyes to how powerful storytelling could be.

In my first job out of college, I was an economist and researcher working at a consulting firm that did class action securities fraud analysis. I analyzed big metadata and did regression analysis for class action lawsuits to determine damage numbers. It was about as interesting as it sounds—which is to say, I would sometimes fall asleep at my desk.

I was so bored. I would stare out at the cars going by, and sometimes, if I got to see a car crash on the highway, that was an exciting day. Most days, to help the time pass, I would read the *New York Times* or listen to National Public Radio. I loved the really personal storytelling on NPR's *This American Life.*

I languished in this job, and one Friday, my boss pulled me into her office and said, "I can see you've been applying for jobs and saving your résumé to the company directory." She kindly relieved me of my position. I left the company with a little bit of severance.

## FIGURING OUT THE NEXT STEP

I got a job at Trader Joe's and saved up money to eventually move from California to New York. In the meantime, I had a lot of time on my hands, so I started taking improv and writing classes. I also started to DJ, and I was trying to get into the public radio space.

In 2009, when I moved to New York, I went through the Upright Citizens Brigade Theatre's improv program and also pursued acting and playwriting. I was immersing myself in the performance world by telling my own stories, writing, and doing improv.

I took a class on storytelling, and it helped me to process a lot of nonsense that occurred in my life. I was able to use these experiences as the source for entertaining stories and began to see them differently. It was great to be part of a creative community, and I started performing in bars and basements all over New York.

At the same time, I was working as a freelance journalist for a small publication and was assigned to write an article about a little community education space that was offering people $30 to teach classes on whatever they were passionate about—beekeeping, calligraphy, stuff like that. The article got a lot of attention, and it gave me the idea to create a storytelling class.

### THE MOTH AND MODERN STORYTELLING

At the time, I started to work part time for The Moth, which was an organization that started in 1997 and was responsible for the revival of modern first-person narrative storytelling. A groundswell of one-person shows erupted. With the advent of the iPod and podcasting, people had a renewed interest in storytelling.

The Moth was expanding to multiple cities, and they had a radio show. People from all over New York City were showing up every night to tell their stories. They had a program to teach storytelling in schools and community centers.

### BRANCHING OUT

After my exposure to storytelling at The Moth and the work I'd done in the comedy and theater world, I was ready to teach a storytelling class. The first class sold out in a week. The second one sold out in a couple days. My classes kept selling out.

About three months into this phase, I got a gig to run a workshop with a small digital ad agency that wanted to hire someone to teach storytelling to their leaders. They were paying what seemed like a huge amount of money for this workshop, and I began to realize what I was charging for my classes up to that point was ludicrously low.

## A NEW TYPE OF STORYTELLING

I developed this workshop from the perspective of performative storytelling, and I wasn't thinking about what would be relevant to storytelling in a business context. In performance settings, people told odd and off-the-wall stories that may not have been "safe for work." I ran the workshop from this perspective, and it was just disastrous. Terrible!

That failure motivated me to learn more about storytelling in a business context. I read book after book. I was getting a really well-rounded view of storytelling from different standpoints—theatrical, comedic, as well as written and fictional standpoints.

## STORYTELLING FOR BUSINESSPEOPLE

Since I'd worked as an economist, I knew about the world of business. I started a class called Storytelling for Businesspeople in 2012, and it sold out pretty quickly. People started asking if I would work with companies and whether I could help them with their pitches and more.

That led me to start coaching individuals; then, about a year later, I started doing workshops within companies. Slowly, the storytelling and coaching became a bigger part of my income. Mind you, I was still working at Trader Joe's but, over time, I went from working there five days a week and doing comedy on the side to teaching more. Finally, in 2014, I transitioned into my storytelling business full time.

### A FEVER BREAKS INTO A NEW CAREER

The day after my birthday that year, I quit my job, then got incredibly sick. I was on the couch with a 105-degree fever. After two or three days, I woke up, and the fever had broken. I was sitting on my couch, looking out the window, thinking, "Well, this is it. I have to do something now."

I sent out emails to drum up business. At first, I taught the classes I had before; then, after a couple months, I got a gig with American Express to teach a workshop. Then a gig with Google. I had been blogging and was gaining some momentum.

My social media was taking off. I was doing a live show. I was putting myself out there. Then, one day in the summer of 2014, NPR interviewed me for the *Morning Edition.* I thought it might result in a couple people calling me about doing some workshops.

### A CRITICAL TURNING POINT

Around that time, I taught a small storytelling class at the Center for Continuing Education in Westchester County. I really didn't think much of it because they paid me next to nothing. It didn't seem like anything momentous.

A couple days after the workshop, a woman who had taken the class emailed me. She said she'd really enjoyed the class and wanted to interview me for a story that she was writing on business and storytelling for the *New York Times*. I said great and spoke with her but, after weeks, I didn't hear anything back.

I just kept doing stuff. I'd had a bunch of false starts, so I wasn't getting my hopes up. That's the nature of entrepreneurship. I experienced a lot of flirtation but no first dates. I kept pushing forward.

### FRONT-PAGE NEWS

I was down in Philadelphia running a workshop, again for no money, when I got a call from the reporter from the *New York Times*. They were going to run the article with my interview, and they wanted to see me in action. The reporter and a photographer came to a workshop I was running in New York the following week. He took some photos of me teaching the class.

Two weeks later, without me noticing, a photo of me was plastered on the front page of the *New York Times* business section teaching my storytelling workshop. After that, everything exploded. I got calls from companies that wanted to fly me to their offices.

### SUCCESS HITS LIKE A TSUNAMI

I went from making like fifteen-thousand dollars per year and eating rice and beans to meeting with CEOs of Fortune

500 companies and talking at conferences. It was surreal. The transformation was so sudden, less like a caterpillar-to-butterfly and more like a tapeworm passing through a terror attack. I could have never anticipated the magnitude.

That great success extended for about a year and a half. Subsequent articles were written. I was doing really well, but bumps in the road were ahead.

I didn't anticipate any of this success. I didn't plan accordingly for tax purposes, and I got a tax bill for twenty-five thousand dollars. For a while, I was dry heaving. I didn't have an accountant at that time, so I had to figure that out. It was tough to go from making fifteen-thousand dollars a year to owing almost twice that in taxes.

## THE COST OF SUCCESS

Other attendant problems came along with my success. Not really in an excessive way, but I was luxuriating in the success because I'd spent so much time working so hard for so little. At the end of 2016 and going into 2017, I really bottomed out. I was close to declaring bankruptcy. I wasn't sure what was going to happen.

I had coasted for a while and run out of new material to share. The marketplace had changed, too. Competitors had entered the storytelling space. Business partnerships fell through. The way that my work was monetized had changed, so money that had been consistent was now less certain. Through relationships with a few clients, I was able to make it through that period.

**TIME TO PIVOT**

That fall, I had this moment of recognition. Some changes were necessary to ensure the future success of my business. I needed to rethink things. I integrated my background in improv and comedy into the storytelling space and broadened the mission of the company to go from helping people tell amazing stories to helping people find their voices.

I rebranded and got some additional people on board. It's been about a year and a half since the rebranding, and I've brought workshops that I used to do for other organizations under my own company umbrella. Now I'm helping people not only tell amazing stories but find their voices and transform their lives. It's a slight change in focus, but it's really meaningful.

**THE TRUE VALUE OF STORYTELLING**

Storytelling is extremely important. Its value in the corporate environment is finally being recognized in a professional way. I've worked with a lot of people to get incredible results, helping them understand the meaning of their journeys and enabling them to leverage their experiences as a way to connect deeply with others.

**EXERCISE: WHAT ARE YOU TOLERATING?**

Take a few minutes and answer these questions in your journal:

- What activities drain you of energy at work? What can you do about them?
- What activities have you considered doing but haven't? What keeps you from taking action?
- List the messages that run through your head when you consider taking action but don't.
  - What is the worst-case scenario if you take action?
  - What's the most likely scenario?
  - What action could you take if either of those scenarios came true?
  - Can you live with that?
- What's one tiny step that you can take today to deal with a situation you've been tolerating? (Examples could be schedule time with your boss, update your résumé, clean your desk, have coffee with a contact, etc.)
- Who can provide you positive, actionable advice to move past your current block? How soon can you talk with them?
- Take a moment to envision what you'd like your life to be like once you've removed or learned to get past the thing you're currently tolerating.
  - What does it feel like?
  - What does the rest of your life look like?

- How much would you like your life to be that way?
- What action will you take today toward creating that reality?

The first step toward a new reality is getting a clear vision of what you'd like your future to look like. You can do it!

# CHAPTER 7

# PLAYING TO WIN:
## Getting the Results
## You Want

---

*If you have built castles in the air, your work
need not be lost; that is where they should
be. Now put the foundations under them.*

−HENRY DAVID THOREAU[26]

## GETTING CLEAR ON WHAT YOU WANT

Often, when I ask my executive coaching clients what they
want, they'll say, "I don't know! And that's my problem."
They always have a little frustration and maybe even a little

---

26  Thoreau, Henry David. *Walden, and on the duty of civil disobedience.*
Thomas Y. Crowell & Company, 1910. p. 357

self-judgment, because they are people who are used to making things happen.

Perhaps you can relate. If you've been used to delaying gratification and putting the needs of your job or your family ahead of your own desires, it's natural that, sometimes, it might be hard to gain clarity on what you want.

Like a radio dial that's in between stations, there may just be too many competing signals interfering with your ability to tune into your own transmission. You may have given so much energy to other priorities that your own broadcast is too weak to make it through to your consciousness.

## BOOSTING YOUR SIGNAL

Never fear. Just as a radio station can boost its signal, you too can find ways to hear your own intentions. I've found that looking back on your best and worst days at work can be a road map to your future satisfaction.

I'd like to take a moment and tell you about two days in my career—one of my best and one of my worst—that have helped me get clear on the things I enjoy and those that tend to suck the energy out of me.

## MY BEST DAY AT WORK

One of my best working days was spent at an advertising photo shoot in an orange grove in Orange County, California. It was January, and the day was an idyllic seventy degrees. The location scout for our shoot had earned her pay. We were shooting under a sheltering oak that hung over the edge of a large pond nestled among rolling hills of fragrant orange trees.

The warm California sun was a welcome respite from the frigid weather of the East Coast I'd left behind. The center of operations for the shoot was a horse stable that was easily twice the size of my home and much more luxurious. I was enjoying the day so thoroughly that I had to keep reminding myself that I was actually getting paid to be there.

Not only was the day fun, but the results were just what we hoped for—brilliant, eye-catching photos for an upcoming ad campaign. Many years later, I can still feel the sun on my face, see the reflection of the majestic oak on the water, smell the fragrance of oranges in the air, and savor the satisfaction of everything coming together just as we'd planned.

I had a perfect workday engaging with a team of incredibly talented people to create something great. What could be better than doing memorable work and having a ball at the same time?

## A BAD DAY FOR THE NEW SHERIFF

Of course, I've had a few bad days too. In the early weeks of a new job where I was hired to lead a divisional marketing team, I ran into a cabal of managers in the business who, prior to my arrival, had been bullying and bossing around the marketing team that now reported to me. Though I needed to work productively with these people, I was not going to allow the bullying to continue. I knew I had to establish new boundaries.

Things came to a head one day in a meeting with this crew when I asked that all requests come to me rather than directly to individuals on my team. As head of the department, it was fully within my authority. However, this group wasn't happy about their loss of power.

Voices were raised and one of the women narrowed her eyes and hissed,

> *"I guess because you're new, you don't know how things work around here."*

Suddenly, I felt I'd been cast in some old western film as the new sheriff in town, and the woman across the table was the black-hatted villain sauntering into the saloon and growling, "Yer not from around these parts, are ya?"

I wanted to laugh at the absurdity of it but didn't dare. I had too much riding on this job. I'd moved my family across five states and nearly a thousand miles for this opportunity. I couldn't fail. I defended the boundaries I'd set up with this group and it was a constant battle, but I kept my eyes open for opportunities to solidify my position. Eventually, due to some other changes within the company and budget cuts, the leverage this group had was diminished.

With that shift, I was able to fully grasp the authority of my position, protect the marketing team, and help them recover from the abuse they'd suffered at the hands of this group. We had a few bruises, but most importantly, we'd learned many valuable lessons.

## THE IMPORTANCE OF USING YOUR POWER

Though I was not a power-hungry leader, I did recognize that I needed to use my given power to keep it. In the case of this standoff, had I acquiesced and allowed their behavior to continue, I would have been abdicating my role as leader of the department.

I would have lost the respect of my team, our marketing efforts would not have been strategic and effective, and I eventually would have lost the confidence of the business leaders. In the short term, I needed to stand my ground or forever be on my heels trying to regain the authority I'd given up in my early days on the job.

## MAINTAINING EQUILIBRIUM AT WORK

I share these stories to give you perspective. Work is work, and expecting that it's always going to be fun and fulfilling is not realistic. But, on the other hand, it's not sustainable to live through day after day of stress and misery.

We must find a balance between activities that are enjoyable and energizing and those that tax your vitality. Unless balance exists, you'll have an energy deficit, which leads to burnout. Recognize when your situation is short-term and has an end date. Discern when you're dealing with a cultural or structural situation where influencing change may be too costly or even futile.

## WHOSE LITTLE VOICE IS THAT?

If you're like most people, you have a little alter ego inside that observes, comments, and critiques everything that you do. I refer to that critic as a gremlin. The gremlin likes to sit on your shoulder and whisper sweet little nothings in your ear. Even though happiness and fulfillment may be important goals for you, they have no meaning for your gremlin.

Your gremlin's job is to protect you by any means necessary. It may tell you not to try, to always take the safe but boring route, or to keep yourself secure by playing small. Your gremlin sees no advantage to risking anything. Its primary objective is one simple thing—survival. Anything beyond just staying alive is irrelevant to your gremlin.

## HOLLYWOOD'S VIEW OF GREMLINS

Most people's gremlins have lot in common with those fuzzy little creatures from the 1984 fantasy film, *Gremlins*. But Hollywood's tips on dealing with gremlins are distinctly different from dealing with gremlins in the real world.

If you haven't seen the movie, here's a quick synopsis. Randall, a struggling inventor, buys a gremlin named Gizmo from a shop in Chinatown. As he's leaving, he is given three ironclad rules that must be strictly adhered to or something bad—but undefined—will happen:

1. Do not expose the gremlin to bright light or it will die.

2. Do not let it get wet.

3. Never feed it after midnight.

Because this is a movie, mischief soon ensues. Through a series of mishaps, Gizmo multiplies, and soon an army of gremlins wreak havoc on the town. The gremlins' crimes range from vandalism to manslaughter. Randall's son, Billy, and his friend recognize that saving the town is up to them.

They hatch a plan that involves a swimming pool, a skylight, and a big explosion to decimate the hordes of evil gremlins. When the dust settles, Gizmo is the only gremlin left, and he is returned to Chinatown where he can be cared for properly without endangering civilization.

## THE IMPORTANT ROLE YOUR GREMLIN PLAYS

Here's how your gremlin may differ from the Hollywood variety:

- Gremlins are not cute and fuzzy like the ones in the movie. In fact, when I envision my gremlin, he looks like he studied actuarial science at college—he's skinny and has a penchant for pleated Dockers khakis and pocket protectors. His glasses are thick and he clears his throat a lot. Fun is a foreign concept to him.

- Gremlins are typically not unhinged. Mine wouldn't say "boo" to a goose. He's extremely conservative and risk-averse. Though he's strong-willed, I don't see him causing chaos for anyone but my sense of fun.

Here's how your gremlin may be like Gizmo and the Hollywood gremlins:

- Though my gremlin is decidedly un-cuddly, he is persistent. He considers himself my protector and is impervious to my hints that he's not welcome. He's like a stray cat that follows you home and meows outside the door until you give him a little milk, then you cannot get rid of him. That's my gremlin.

- Like the Hollywood gremlins, if you feed your gremlin's doubts when things get dark, it only gets bigger and stronger. Likewise, when I pay attention to my gremlin, his negative messages multiply like poisonous weeds and are just as caustic.

- When I shine light on my gremlin, he tends to shrink (but not fully perish). He doesn't like it when I pick apart his conspiracy theories. My gremlin is unmoved if I bring facts, likelihoods, and past positive experiences to bear in countering his arguments. He wants to stay strong and to keep me frozen.

- When I tried to kill my gremlin, it backfired, and his whispers became screams and shouts until I couldn't hear myself think. Like Gizmo, gremlins need to be cared for properly so they can coexist with their hosts.

## NAMING YOUR GREMLIN

I've come up with a different way of dealing with my gremlin. The first step was to name him. I call mine Ralph. For many years, he didn't have a name. He was just a voice whispering in my ear, and I sometimes mistook his voice for my own inner wisdom.

But after I named Ralph, it was easy to see him for what he was—a well-meaning part of myself who tried his best to keep me safe through fear-based arguments.

Though Ralph is annoying and neurotic, I've decided to embrace him and recognize that he's looking out for me because he loves me, and he knows no other way to show it. He doesn't assign any value to my desire to have more fun, explore, and feel joy.

When he pulls the graphing calculator out of his pristine pocket protector and does the math, to him, the odds aren't worth any risk. Now I tell Ralph that I hear and appreciate him, but I am respectfully going my own way.

Since I recognized Ralph's just trying to keep me safe in a blunt way, I learned that the physiological symptoms of fear are the same as excitement, and it's actually how we view the sensations that make them seem pleasant or unpleasant.

## A CALMING MANTRA

I've developed new ways to view my discomfort when I need to take action that scares me. To quell my anxiety, I adopted a new mantra of "say yes to adventure." The mantra calms me until I focus on my goals without giving Ralph much heed. All it took to tame him was giving him a name, embracing him as part of myself, and changing the lens through which I viewed the sensations I felt. Turns out, he's a good little gremlin after all.

## MANAGING YOUR GREMLIN

You have your own gremlin. If you find that you're holding yourself back from what you want because of perceived risk, it may be that your gremlin has more control over you than it needs to. Here are a few questions to help you make a distinction between your own inner wisdom and your nervous-Nelly gremlin that wants to keep you safe at all costs, even when the likelihood of danger is slim.

- **What is your gremlin's name?** Part of embracing your gremlin is naming it so that you can distinguish this single-minded safety monitor from your wiser self. This way, you can talk to it like you would a rather simple friend. "Yes, Leonard, I appreciate your concern about the risks associated with taking on this new project. I have thought this through and have decided that the likely rewards outweigh the potential pitfalls. I would appreciate your support as I move ahead. Let me know if you see any new risks as I proceed."

- **What are three examples of times when you've done something that you were afraid to do and it worked out well?** Did everything go exactly according to plan? If not, how did you deal with the problems that arose?

- **How able are you to distinguish the voice of your gremlin from your inner wisdom?** Your gremlin's message is always tinged with a little fear, drama, and worst-case scenarios. It's okay to listen, but allow the wise part of yourself to evaluate the points that the gremlin brings up and decide intentionally—rather than based on fear—what action to take.

- **What is the worst-case scenario?** What's the likelihood that it will happen? Is it something that you can live with? What are your options if it does happen?

- **What's the best-case scenario?** What's the most likely scenario? Is the risk of the worst-case scenario worth taking a chance to achieve the best-case or most likely scenario? As you've heard many times before, no risk, no reward. Rarely do people make progress without some risk.

- **What can you do to mitigate any risk that your gremlin uncovers?** For example, if you'd like to apply for a promotion, but you're not sure if you're qualified, who can help you understand the requirements of the job? I often encourage my clients to have informational interviews with people doing jobs they are interested in. In the vast majority of cases, my clients are pleasantly surprised at how informative and enjoyable the conversations are.

- **How can you embrace your gremlin and be grateful that part of you is looking out for your best interest?** Consider times when your gremlin brought an issue to your attention that caused you to make a better decision. You don't need to follow the instructions of your gremlin in all cases, but often people find that if they are willing to listen openly and recognize that its exhortations are coming from a place of keeping them safe, they have less fear than if they try to repress the messages.

## BEING RESPONSIBLE FOR WHAT YOU WANT

Any time you want something, examine your own commitment to your goal. Sometimes you may be giving yourself mixed messages. Perhaps your deepest desire is to pursue a particular goal, but your gremlin is sending you a message that drains you of energy.

A tug-of-war is taking place subconsciously. By the time the desire rises to your level of consciousness, you feel exhausted and demoralized before you even consider taking action. If so, your gremlin has more control than it deserves.

## DO YOU DESERVE THE THINGS YOU WANT?

I'd like to use an example that many clients share—the desire to be promoted. One of the first things that I'll ask is: "Do you deserve a promotion?" Admittedly, that's a loaded question. People typically respond to this question in three ways. Let's see how each of these characters deals with it:

- **Donny Defensive** rattles off all the reasons he deserves it and everything he's done that is not being recognized.

- **Cathy Confident** is calm and self-assured, stating something like, "Yes, I understand what the expectations are for promotion, and I've fulfilled them. I deserve a promotion."

- **Alan Aspirer** says, "This is an aspiration. I believe I have the potential to be successful at the next level, but I'm not sure what's required."

Each one of these responses reflects the beliefs of the individual and has big implications for what they'll do next, the likelihood they'll get the promotion, and their chances of success at the next level.

## GETTING IN THE MIND-SET FOR PROMOTION

Generally, it's management who decides who gets promoted, but I'd argue that management doesn't decide who deserves promotion. Only you can decide whether you deserve it or not. It's really a matter of mind-set. Energy theory tells us that energy attracts similar energy.

### DONNY'S MIND-SET

In the three scenarios above, we encounter different types of energy and mind-set at work. In the first scenario, Donny Defensive is coming from a position of lack—waiting for someone else to recognize the value he brings and tap him on the shoulder to pull him up to the next level.

He's yearning for external validation. Something of the martyr complex is at work here. He wants recognition but doesn't want to fully take on the responsibility associated with his desire for productive action. Donny may fear that, if he commits and tries, he'll fail and won't be able to live with that view of himself.

### CATHY'S MIND-SET

In the second scenario, Cathy Confident has explored what the organization values and has taken responsibility for delivering results that line up with the expectations. She understands the value that she brings. She is willing to step up fully and have her contributions judged.

She might have miscalculated or may not judge her contributions in the same way as her boss, but she is not playing the victim as Donny does. One of the benefits of this perspective is that Cathy's view of herself is stable regardless of whether it is validated by those outside herself. She may be disappointed if she doesn't get the promotion, but she won't doubt herself.

She is a true leader because she believes herself to be. She acts as if her desired state has already happened. This often results in others seeing her potential and in her ambition being fulfilled. Taking responsibility for her mindset frees Cathy from the tyranny of what other people may think of her. If a promotion doesn't come from her current employer, Cathy can more easily preserve her self-confidence and see opportunities where her goal can be fulfilled.

### ALAN'S MIND-SET

The third scenario with Alan Aspirer is similar to the second scenario. It's simply a matter of how far into the goal setting and exploration process Alan is. Alan has a goal but recognizes he doesn't yet know how to fulfill it.

Because it's early in the process, Alan doesn't know what he doesn't know. He has mustered the courage to say what he wants—a promotion. To explore what he'll need to do to be ready, he may undertake research, side projects, volunteering, or informational interviews to gain clarity.

After he's gathered more information and his goal becomes clear, he can discover the gaps between where he is currently and where he'd like to go. Alan may choose to brainstorm with an experienced friend, mentor, or coach on how to fill those gaps.

He can ask others in the role how critical the various skill and experience gaps are. How did they learn? What's critical to know beforehand and what can be learned on the job?

Similar to Cathy, Alan must take responsibility for developing a plan and executing it if he's committed to getting to his goal. Waiting for someone else to take him there could result in no action or finding himself in a role that he has no interest in.

## GETTING CLEAR ON YOUR GOALS

To create a career you're happy with, it's critical to develop a clear goal and build a plan to accomplish it. Not doing so is like allowing yourself to be blown by the wind, then feeling like the victim when you find yourself in a place you don't like. This approach is a sure ticket to stagnation and dissatisfaction.

The subconscious mind cannot tell the difference between reality and dreams. If you can envision a clear picture of what a promotion will be like and how you'll act, look, and be, you will begin to live that way. As a result, others will begin to see you that way as well.

Make no mistake, this does not happen "auto-magically"—you don't just sit around thinking this stuff (and doing nothing else) and get a big raise and promotion dropped in your lap.

But when you mentally create the future environment in your mind, you begin to see opportunities, and if you act on them, it sets other things in motion that will move you toward your goal.

When you envision yourself at that next level already, suddenly investing in a wardrobe upgrade makes sense. You identify and address skill gaps proactively by seeking training, mentoring, and coaching. You take responsibility for your own career rather than holding fast to the myth that some all-powerful manager has control over whether you advance or not.

## RIDING THE BOSS'S COATTAILS

Some people attach themselves to their boss's coattails, believing that's the path to advancement. They adapt their career approach to their manager's style, and this can work nicely for a while. But if that manager leaves and doesn't take the employee with them, that approach likely won't work so well with the new manager, particularly if they have a different style or different plans for the department.

When this is the strategy, the employee is caught flat-footed without a plan B because he abdicated responsibility for his advancement to his former boss. (This happened to me when my promised promotion at my first job walked out with my boss, Dennis, when he was fired. The new boss felt no obligation to follow through on that promotion, and he didn't.)

You have the ability to add value, you are here on earth for a reason, and you are the one who ultimately decides if you deserve it. Even if you don't have a path to career advancement at your current employer, if you believe you are worthy, then act like you are, and you will find the opportunities, and they may even find you.

## SUPERHERO SYNDROME

"I'm not happy with how my job is going. At every job I've had, I'm expected to fix my coworkers' problems," Jessica said. "I'm tired of being the hero."

Jessica was a potential coaching client telling me about her job. She had once loved it, but now the job was just a heavy burden and the cause of burnout. She was discouraged, but in five words, Jessica gave me the key to help her overcome her work troubles.

Perhaps you've been there. You long for more from your job. More autonomy, more recognition, more rewards . . . more satisfaction! You want to be seen as ready for the next level, but no matter what you do, it seems like the movie *Groundhog Day*.

## IT'S NOT FAIR!

Your boss selects someone else for advancement and you're left with the same responsibilities you mastered ages ago. It doesn't seem fair because you consistently go above and beyond, even bailing out coworkers on a regular basis. Without you, it's clear that the place would fall apart. Doesn't the boss see that?

You may be wondering which five words helped pinpoint Jessica's issue—they were:

*"At every job I've had."*

These few words told me that the issue was not with Jessica's boss or coworkers or even the culture of the company. The problem was with Jessica. How do I know this for certain? Well, because the one common factor in all her jobs was Jessica.

## STOP CRYING IN YOUR BEER

If you're experiencing a similar situation, you may not want to consider yourself the root of the problem. After all, why doesn't the boss do something, or why can't the coworkers learn to do their jobs better? You may be thinking it's unfair that you have to change because others won't. And you are one-hundred percent correct.

*Cry a little, moan a little . . . are you done?*

Now get over it!

Life is not fair and work, especially, is not fair. This really gets at the heart of the purpose of the book. Work is a game, and we can act as if it's not. We can refuse to see what's really going on and instead whine about "how it should be" or "how it used to be."

## NO ENERGY IN "VICTIM MODE"

When we sit around whining about unfairness, we stay stuck in victim mode with no energy to make much-needed changes. When we accept that we cannot change others and the only change we have control over is with ourselves, we become truly empowered.

If you feel like you're expected to save everyone around you, it's likely your issue lies with a belief that got lodged in your mind long ago—so long ago that you don't even realize it's there. Deep down, the belief is likely a variation of, "I'm not enough on my own," or "My worth is dependent on helping others." You have superhero syndrome.

## STOP RESCUING AND FOCUS ON PRIORITIES

If you've had enough and finally want to change things for good, here are seven steps to help you recover from your superhero syndrome:

1. Clarify your own work priorities. Write them down and keep them in a place you can see them.

2. For one full week, review your priority list first thing each day and get to work on them. Don't let habit or distractions get in your way.

3. At the end of each day, review your priorities and see how you've done. Give yourself a grade, and if it's anything less than a B+, make note of what kept you from scoring higher. The next day, do your best to address the issues that kept you from focusing on your priorities. Keep it up each day until you see improvement.

4. Learn this powerful word—no. When coworkers interrupt you or ask for your help on things that are not your priority, practice saying no in its many variations:

- "No, I'm sorry."
- "I can't now. Maybe later."
- "I'm very busy today."
- "Try Googling it."
- "I can't. Perhaps someone else can help you."
- "I'm on a deadline."

5. If you have trouble sticking with your plan, ask yourself what underlying belief is causing you to want to give up or jump into making other people's priorities your own. Journal about the benefits you'll enjoy from focusing on your work instead of everyone else's needs. Talk with a trusted (nonwork) friend, counselor, or coach about any discomfort you're feeling about the change. Try to stick with it despite your discomfort.

6. When the week is up, check in with yourself to gauge your satisfaction. Overall, how well were you able to focus on your own priorities? How do you feel? How much work did you complete compared to a typical week? What else happened as result of your changes?

7. If the results were good, try it for another week and recognize the impact you could have by continuing to focus your efforts on your own priorities. Employees responsible for positive impact tend to get rewarded. By conserving your own energy for your priorities—rather than those of your coworkers—you should be able to focus on areas of importance for you.

## TOLERATING THE DISCOMFORT OF CHANGE

For some, I realize that merely the thought of saying no can bring on a cold sweat, but that's a sign change is long overdue.

You will need to tolerate discomfort for a little while until you get used to it. Discomfort won't kill you—you'll survive. If you want to change your situation, discomfort is necessary and healthy.

Over time, you'll find your discomfort at not jumping in to rescue others will fade. You'll begin to see that when you don't prop others up, they either learn how to function on their own or their ineptitude becomes apparent and the boss makes a decision about whether they're a fit for the role they're in.

While it may be hard to see someone be demoted or even lose their job, you must remember that each person is responsible for their own duties.

When you overstep the boundaries of your own job to do someone else's, you're overburdening yourself and also clouding your manager's ability to see who is actually delivering value. Wouldn't you prefer to conserve some of your energy for your own life or for your own projects that gain you recognition than to prop up a coworker?

## THE ANSWER YOU'RE SEEKING IS IN YOU

With the lessons of this chapter, you can think differently about what you do each day and decide whether you're getting the results you'd like. It can be easy to look for reasons outside yourself for the results you're getting. I'm not saying that others don't have any control over or impact on your professional success, but the only control you have is over your own behavior.

If you don't like the results you're seeing, use some of the tools I've shared in this chapter to shift your mindset. Try to see your situation from a different perspective and experiment with new behaviors to see if you can get results that align more with your expectations.

Good luck! I know you can do it.

# ANDREW, PART 2: WE ARE OUR STORIES

———

You met Andrew Linderman earlier in the book when he shared how he washed out of corporate America on a wave of pure boredom. Eventually, his passion for theater and improv led him to found his company, The Story Source, which helps professionals learn to tell their own stories to connect with themselves and others in a human way.

I decided to provide more space for Andrew to share his views on storytelling because they align so well with the mission of this book—to help you know yourself better and live and work more authentically. As Andrew so wisely puts it, we are our stories.

## IN HIS OWN WORDS

People don't pay you for who you are. They pay you for the value you can create for them. However, I don't think people can be different from who they are innately. This is true for everybody in my family and it's true for me—I can't be anyone but myself. I tried working a job that was not for me, and I couldn't get out fast enough. By that, I mean I got fired.

### REMAINING TRUE TO MYSELF

From the time I was a kid, if I didn't want to do something, it wasn't going to happen. I was incapable of doing something that didn't appeal to me. I just couldn't do it.

What I realize as a business owner is that, when you're your own boss, you're also everyone else's employee. I thought people would pay for me, but they're not paying for *me*. They're paying for an experience that I create for them. Running my own business has allowed me to be myself and be true to who I am.

As I create a space for customers to learn and grow, I learn from my customers and I also grow. It allows me to be the best version of myself. That's been the biggest benefit to me, even more important than money.

### AN ENTREPRENEURIAL LEGACY

As an entrepreneur, I learned a lot from my family. My dad started out on a career path to become a partner in a law firm, but he couldn't conform to that legal corporate culture, and that caused problems for him. He ended up getting fired from a couple of jobs for his personality quirks.

My dad had this entrepreneurial side to him that seems to have been passed down genetically. My dad's grandfather was a tailor and an immigrant from Eastern Europe. My dad's dad owned discotheques back in the 1960s, and his mom was a writer, so they were independent folks.

### DAD BECOMES THE ICE CREAM MAN

My dad was let go from a job in law and for two years owned and ran an ice cream shop. Some may look at being an entrepreneur as a dream, but for my dad, it quickly became a waking nightmare. Ice cream is a fair-weather business in every sense of the phrase.

This wasn't his dream. He had lost his job and needed to run the business to have income. The economy was going into recession in the early 1990s, and he was lucky to sell it for a small profit.

### UNDERSTANDING YOUR STORY

People out in the world are depressed because they are not expressing who they truly are. They feel trapped. The key to turning that around is about getting clear on who they truly are and redefining what success looks like specifically for them.

You may think that, if you quit a job you don't like, then life will be great, but you're still the same person. You chose that job. If things are to change, it's not about the job. It's about you. What are you going to do differently?

## WE ARE OUR STORIES

Storytelling helps us tap into our potential to change our trajectories. You get to examine the things that got you where you are, for better or worse, and to reframe the narrative so you can create a future for yourself grounded in the essence of your values. We are our stories. Whatever story you're in will give you the results of that story down the line. You need that story to evolve if you want things to be different.

A lot of times, people think they know who they are, but really, they've spent a lot of time defining themselves in a somewhat narrow capacity. The work I do is oriented around pressing people to expand the things they truly care about and value. I don't mean that in a hokey way, but in terms of what they are looking to create.

## IT'S NOT ABOUT WHAT YOU'RE NOT

People often define themselves in kind of an antithetical way. They talk about what they aren't rather than what they are. People will say, "I'm not a corporate person," but they haven't necessarily thought about what they *are*.

What have they offered? That's the question. People often can easily identify what they don't want, but it's harder to say what they do want. They spend so much time trying to figure out what somebody else wants from them and conforming to that vision so they will be tapped for some big job, but then they get it and have lost themselves.

## THOUGHTS BECOME REALITY

Our thoughts are energy that go toward the creation of some future outcome. What are you looking to create? The results of the actions you're taking will be what you bring into the world.

A lot of people draw a blank when presented with that question because much of what they've spent their time creating has been on the surface. Their tension and unhappiness comes, deep down, from not feeling personally aligned with their goals.

When boiled down, money is a placeholder for value. What is the basis for this trade you're making? Because you've got to recognize that you're always trading. Are you trading something that has meaning for you? What's the purpose behind the trade?

## HOW TO REGAIN YOUR MOJO

If you want different results, you have to take different actions. If you want to take different actions, you have to have different intentions. To have different intentions, things have to occur to you differently. For them to occur to you differently, you have to be different. This is not "fake it until you make it," it's "*be* it so you *are* it."

To become personally alive, you have to delve back into the moments where you were deeply connected to what you were doing and the people around you. Then you can use that as a jumping-off point for what you're trying to create. It's about going deep into moments of connection and using those moments as sources of inspiration for the next chapter of your life.

## WHY STORYTELLING IS IMPORTANT

That gets us back to the meaning of storytelling. You have to take an honest assessment to understand who you are so you can understand where you're going. This means you need to rewrite your story, because when you look at your own narrative, you think it means a certain thing.

You may be looking at it through someone else's filter or through what you've been told to think. You can become really attached to that narrative, and because that's your story and nothing is changing, you just keep getting the same results. It always ends the same way.

## A DIFFERENT STORY LEADS TO A DIFFERENT RESULT

A lot of people's stories are holding them down. You can only be yourself. You can't change that, but you can change the stories you tell yourself.

For example, a person can look back and say,

"I've been abused and I can't go forward."

They might use that as an excuse for holding on to limitations in their life. But if they were to turn that around and give it different meaning, they could change what comes after that.

Realize you *can* do this, but not only that, you *need* to do this, because if you don't, then you're going to get left behind, living out a story that you aren't happy with.

Your identity is attached to whatever story you currently believe about yourself. Whatever your story is today doesn't have to be your story forever. As things change around you, that narrative needs to evolve as well.

## FINDING YOUR OWN PATH

When you do step away from the well-worn path, you create your own. When you're hacking out your path with a machete, occasionally you will fall into a gulley. You may be sidelined for a while as you recover, but then you hike back up to the path and get back on it. Some people take those pitfalls as signs they aren't on the right path, but in reality, it's just all part of their individual journey.

It's worth it to me to take that risk and have the freedom. I was out there with the machete at times because of where my business was. For me, it's only fun to be in the jungle where I'm finding my own way. I carve my own unique path. I don't traipse down some path that someone else created. That's important to me. Pitfalls are just part of it.

## NEW FACTORS LEAD TO NEW OUTCOMES

A lot of people leave their corporate jobs because they think being an entrepreneur is sexy. When I left the corporate world and started my own business, people envied me. They'd be like,

*"You don't have to deal with the corporate BS.*
*You're so lucky.*
*You can go hike this mountain."*

But when you're an entrepreneur, it's a commitment. You have to keep doing what needs to be done, even when it's no longer as much fun. That's how my dad was at first with his ice cream store.

When I told my friends my dad owned an ice cream store, they thought I was the coolest kid and they wanted to be friends. Then winter came and it was cold, and nobody was around, and we earned no money. He still had to show up and try to sell ice cream.

### GETTING CLEAR ON THE *WHY* OF WHAT YOU DO

When my business was going well, I had a girlfriend. Everything seemed great. But a couple tumbles into the ditch, the girl and the money were gone and the apartment was in limbo. You have to really ask yourself how much you want it. What do you really care about?

Most people don't fully anticipate what a lifestyle change will mean for their whole life. Everything won't be the same just because they don't have to take the early train to work every day or deal with their jerk of a boss.

### RESPONDING WITH ACCEPTANCE AND GRATITUDE

When I tell the story of my first write-up in the *New York Times*,[27] it sounds so great to people. It's a funny thing, but I was angry, not because I didn't appreciate it. I was angry

---

27  Tugend, Alina. *"Storytelling Your Way to a Better Job or a Stronger Start-Up."* New York Times, December 12, 2014.

because I was like, "Where were you when I had no money? I'd been advocating for years. Where were you then?"

What I ultimately realized is that it isn't about me. If they're going to write about me, it's about what I'm creating. I'm going to be on this journey regardless. I should have gratitude and appreciation for anyone who's going to help lift me up to make whatever I'm doing bigger.

You've got to be satisfied with what you're doing, regardless of how other people respond to it. You can't have that kind of resentment; you just have to make peace with what is. You have to be happy with the journey that you're on, even if it's not the one other people are on. You have to find solace in that.

### DISCOVERING YOUR PURPOSE

We are each here for a reason. The ultimate journey is about becoming fully who we are meant to be. People who are really successful tap into that. It's a lifelong journey, really. The more time you spend holding on to those external things, the farther you may have to fall to walk up a different path. There's a zen quality that you have to practice to thrive in the environment.

### BE TRUE TO YOURSELF AND REWARD THE WORLD

I wish I had absorbed that lesson earlier. I have tremendous gratitude for my ability to do this day-in and day-out, to be where I am, and to bring other people into the fold. When you do things for yourself, from your authentic core, you are really doing things for the world.

## EXERCISE: WHAT'S YOUR STORY?

Spend some time writing the story of your career. Go back as far as you can to the seed of your current career. Write about yourself in third person (he/she/they) rather than first person. When you read the story back to yourself, you may receive some insights because you're able to get a little distance from your experience.

Here are some questions to get you started:

- What is the earliest memory you have of your motivation to pursue your current career?
- What were the influences that caused you to pursue your career?
- What have been your biggest accomplishments?
- What have been your biggest failures?
- What fulfills you the most about what you do for a living?
- Examine the key pivot points in your career and write down the factors that influences the changes you made.
- If you could do it all over again, would you do it the same way? If not, what changes would you make?
- How authentically does your profession reflect who you are inside? If you see gaps, how could they be bridged?
- What's the meaning of your story?
- What's the moral of your story?

- Is it a story of triumph, a cautionary tale, or something else altogether?
- If your story were a movie, who would play you?
- Are you happy with the direction of your story?
- Is it a comedy, a tragedy, or something in between?
- Is your story headed for a happy ending or does it need a rewrite?

After you've completed your story, let it sit for a couple days, then go back and read it. You may even want to let a close friend or family member read it as well and share their insights. Journal about the trends and patterns you notice in your story and how it makes you feel.

# PART 3

# TAKING YOUR GAME TO THE NEXT LEVEL

## CHAPTER 8

# BECOMING YOUR OWN AGENT: Understanding And Leveraging Your Value

———

*Joy, feeling one's own value, being appreciated and loved by others, feeling useful and capable of production are all factors of enormous value for the human soul.*

—MARIA MONTESSORI[28]

---

28  Montessori, Maria. Brainyquote.com. Accessed February 2, 2020.

Often you may not recognize things about yourself that others can see clearly. As I'm fond of saying,

> *"You can't read the label when*
> *you're inside the bottle."*

The purpose of this chapter is to provide you with perspective and resources that will help you see yourself the way others see you.

When you understand how you're viewed, you can make intentional changes so your self-image and the image you project are much more aligned. This is the first step to being compensated for the value you provide to your organization.

## LESSONS FROM HGTV

I'm going to confess a deep, dark secret . . . I'm a sucker for HGTV. I love settling in for marathons of *House Hunters, Property Brothers, Fixer Upper,* and scores of other real estate shows. I find something strangely appealing about watching people search for their dream home in Malibu or renovate their mid-century modern in Kansas City.

I won't call it a guilty pleasure, because after hundreds of hours of HGTV, I've learned a valuable career lesson. Buyers abhor uncertainty and will put off buying or require a big discount to overcome any perceived risk.

## YOU'RE ALWAYS SELLING

If you're wondering what "buying" has to do with your career, it's simple. Anytime you're trying to influence someone—be it your boss, a colleague, or the hiring manager at a company you aspire to work for—you're selling, and they need to buy in order for you to achieve your goal.

Getting hired is an important sales job. Bringing on a new employee, like buying a house, can be fraught with risk. Organizations make a significant investment when they hire a new employee. Interviewing takes time. When a candidate is hired, they need to be trained and introduced to the people they'll work with.

They may need to meet and form relationships with clients. And all this happens before the new employee ever starts creating value for the company. If the new hire doesn't work out, a lot of effort and political capital will have been wasted.

## "I JUST NEED A CHANCE!"

I've heard this refrain hundreds of times: "All I need is for someone to take a chance on me—once they hire me, they'll see I was worth the risk." I've said these same words myself at times in my career. It was frustrating when I was ready to move up and I couldn't seem to get my foot in the door.

However, I understood it much more clearly once I became a manager. Given what is at stake for the manager, most aren't keen on taking chances without ample evidence it will pay off. Even if you are able to do a particular job, your résumé needs to say that clearly.

For most managers, they want some assurances that the person they're considering has at least some experience similar to the job they are hiring for. Even when a candidate has had similar responsibilities at another company, it's often hard to get clarity on the intangibles like work ethic, cultural fit, and the quality of their work.

## PROVE IT TO ME

Some of my worst hiring mistakes were when I convinced myself that someone was a good bet rather than making them convince me. I gave them the benefit of the doubt rather than insisting they prove to me that they were worthy of my trust and confidence. When I look back, I recognize that I had some reservations, but I didn't delve deeper when I should have.

I was anxious to get the roles filled and get on with the normal routine. Only later did I realize that I'd let my own impatience or optimism cloud my judgment. This would be analogous to buying a house and taking the homeowner's word that there were no problems with the furnace rather than consulting a home inspector to confirm it.

## CREATING CAREER CURB APPEAL

Enter the lessons from the HGTV gurus! When a homeowner is trying to sell a home on those programs, professionals advise the seller to get their property ready for the market by creating curb appeal—clean it up, declutter, paint, cut the grass, get new carpet, and even pay a company to stage the home.

This allows the home to be shown to potential buyers in the best possible light. It eliminates the need for potential buyers to overlook the stains on the carpet or the neglected garden. When a home looks like it's "move-in ready," buyers are inclined to believe what they see and want to buy.

## "AS IS" REQUIRES A LEAP OF FAITH

Alternately, when homeowners list their homes "as is" and make no investment in fixing up the home before listing it, it is typically sold at a big discount. The uncertainty of potential problems is priced in.

The beauty of many programs on HGTV is that experienced real estate and building professionals will examine a fixer-upper and can tell if the issue is just cosmetic or if it's an expensive fix. Your average buyer doesn't have the time or expertise to do that and therefore shies away from buying "as is" homes. They just want to close, move in, and get on with their lives.

Most hiring managers don't have time to examine each candidate's potential in any depth. They are like the home buyer that just wants to buy a "move-in ready" house.

Taking time to hire a new employee is a huge disruption from their day-to-day job. The last thing a manager wants to do is invest time and effort to hire someone, then not have them work out. The consequences could be costly in both lost productivity and reputation.

## DON'T SELL YOURSELF SHORT

When you're looking for a job, make your value and attractiveness immediately visible on your résumé and LinkedIn profile. When you get a screening interview, be ready with clear examples of how you've been successful in previous roles that align with the job.

Be sure to bring the energy as well. Many managers will choose to hire someone who really wants a job over a slightly more qualified candidate who doesn't show a high level of interest in the position. Blasé is not a good look when you're serious about getting a job.

## INVEST TO REDUCE PERCEIVED RISK

What can you do if you want to pivot to something new or you're a new graduate who doesn't have any professional experience? Invest in yourself to reduce the perceived risk of hiring you.

Here are a few things that you can do to gain career curb appeal:

- Learn to tell your story in a concise and compelling way.
- Spruce up your résumé.
- Get your LinkedIn profile to all-star status.
- Get some additional training in areas where you have gaps.
- Make sure your image fits the role that you're aiming for. Invest in a stylist if needed.

If you're not sure what blocks stand in the way of your career goals, hire a professional. Like a realtor advising a homeowner on getting their home to appeal to the largest number of buyers, a career coach can help you get yourself ready for the job market so you're also in demand.

## TRYING TO GET HIRED "AS IS"

Years ago, when my boss left the large bank we worked for, I applied for his job. I had been his right-hand person and was heavily involved in the operations of the department and the interactions with leaders in the business. In the months after he left, I stepped up to provide leadership to the team and felt that I had a good shot at being officially promoted into the role.

## ASSUMPTIONS CAN LEAD TO BIG MISTAKES

I applied for the role, but I didn't do anything special to prepare myself for the interview. I had been at the company for about eight years at that point and would be interviewing with people who I had worked with in different capacities over the years. I assumed they understood the value I brought to the organization. In retrospect, that was my big mistake.

Because most of the interviewers supported other businesses and were in another city, they actually didn't understand what I did. Their knowledge of my expertise and contributions was shallow. In addition, I hadn't interviewed in the eight years since the company hired me.

## A CRUSHING HUMILIATION

The first interview was with human resources and was basically a screening interview. I did well enough to be granted a second interview. The second-round interview was with a panel of marketing leaders from other areas of the company. I had never been in a panel interview before and wasn't sure what to expect. Disappointingly, in the interview, I became anxious and didn't perform well. Let's just call it what it was—I bombed!

I felt so humiliated, not only because I hadn't presented myself in my best light, but also because I would continue to work with and see these people at departmental events. I felt like they would be looking at me as a lightweight and unworthy of performing at a management level. It was embarrassing.

## GETTING PROFESSIONAL HELP

Frankly, I don't like viewing myself as less than an all-star. Though I realized I wouldn't be progressing to the next phase of the interview process, I was motivated to get at the heart of my disastrous performance.

I hired a career coach to help me get over my interview anxiety. With her help, I learned how to talk naturally and persuasively about the value that I brought to the organization. I used the **PAR method** to concisely frame up:

- The **problems** I encountered.
- The **actions** I took.
- The **results** I delivered.

## GOING FROM "AS IS" TO "AS IF"

My career coach also helped me recognize how to package myself so employers would see me as ready to deliver value at the next level. I went on a shopping spree and bought some suits and dresses that were more tailored and higher-quality than what I typically wore to work. I was dressing for the job I wanted rather than the job I was currently in. I started acting "as if" I were already at that next level.

The recruiting process for the open role continued; eventually, a candidate was offered the position, but she declined to take the job. The hiring manager didn't feel comfortable offering the role to any of the other candidates, so he started the recruiting process again from square one.

## DISAPPOINTMENT TURNS TO HOPE

I reapplied for the role and, using the skills and new mindset I'd practiced with the help of my coach, I progressed to the final round of interviews. It was down to me and an external candidate. I felt much more confident going through the process the second time, and I was able to easily communicate the value that I provided for the organization. I was hopeful that this time I'd earn the promotion.

Unfortunately, it wasn't meant to be. When I found out they offered the role to the external candidate, I was disappointed. But it didn't take long to realize that the universe had a different plan for me. The day I learned that the other candidate had accepted the job, while I was at lunch, a recruiter left a voicemail about a role that was a great fit for me at another company.

## PERSISTENCE PAYS OFF

It was as if I was being told that, since I'd prepared, something bigger was in store—and indeed there was. That message began an active period of interviewing. By the time I finally moved on from that company, I had two job offers and was actively interviewing with a third company.

The investment I made in improving my skills and promoting myself mentally to the next level resulted in the outcome I'd been seeking. Instead of naively expecting people to see me the way I saw myself, I learned to present myself in a way that made them feel confident "buying" and gave them no doubt that any investment in me would be worth it. The investment I made in myself paid off.

## SEEING YOURSELF THROUGH A NEW LENS

If you've got big goals and you're not getting the response you expect, take an inventory of how you're perceived. Many companies offer 360-degree feedback surveys for employees.

People who have interacted with the employee—peers, superiors, direct reports, and sometimes vendors and customers—will be asked to anonymously answer a series of questions about how they perceive the employee. The employee is given a report with the results to help them increase self-awareness.

If a company-sponsored 360-degree survey is not an option for you, you can get feedback in several ways:

- **Ask friends or colleagues** who will be straight with you how you're viewed. Obviously, this approach could be uncomfortable for you and those you're asking and may not result in fully honest feedback.

- **Create a version of your own 360-degree survey** using SurveyMonkey and provide the link to friends and colleagues so they can give you anonymous feedback on how you're perceived.

- **Many executive coaches and career coaches offer this service** and can conduct a 360-degree survey on your behalf. The benefit of this approach is that they provide some context for the feedback and work with you on a development plan to address any skill gaps or behavior changes that are needed.

## FEEDBACK IS A GIFT

The feedback you get isn't always easy to digest if it's different than what you expected, but recognize that feedback is a gift. People already think what they will of you, and it's only when they share their views that you have any chance of changing a negative perception.

It's much better to get it from people who know and care about you than to squander opportunities because you're not showing up at your potential best. Having an objective supporter in your corner can also be helpful in maintaining a healthy perspective as you work on bridging any gaps.

Just as an experienced realtor can help you see flaws in your own home that should be addressed before putting it on the market, a mentor or coach can help you refine how you present yourself, whether it be for a new job or a promotion.

In the aftermath of my botched interview, brushing up on my interviewing skills was awkward and nerve-wracking, but the discomfort was worth it. Though it was uncomfortable to face how I was perceived, afterward I felt much more confident and able to showcase my capabilities.

## MORE RESPONSIBILITY WITHOUT MORE PAY

Let's switch gears to another problem that sometimes crops up in the workplace. In some ways, taking on more responsibility without more pay is the opposite of seeking a promotion. You are perceived as competent—maybe so competent that you can take on much more responsibility—but with one little catch. You get more responsibility without a raise! Here's a story of how this situation began for me.

My boss asked me to have breakfast with the head of sales for another division in our company. I wasn't told the reason for the meeting, but it seemed suspiciously like a job interview. Sure enough, a week or so after the breakfast meeting, my boss asked me to take on responsibility for that division's marketing team in addition to my current role leading marketing for another business.

## EXCITEMENT FADES TO CONCERN

I was excited about the opportunity for advancement, but I soon realized I needed to slow my roll. My boss explained that, though my responsibilities were doubling, I would be given no raise, only a vague promise to consider a mid-year bonus based on undefined performance results.

Soon an announcement went out to the entire marketing organization, making it sound like I'd gotten a promotion. I honestly wasn't sure how to respond when people began to congratulate me. "Thanks . . . I guess?" The pats on the back and congratulatory emails from colleagues just reinforced the nagging feeling that something wasn't quite right with this situation.

## MORE WORK FOR THE SAME PAY

With economic disruption in many industries, this scenario has become increasingly common. I have heard many examples of employees being asked to take on substantially more responsibility without the benefit of a raise, formal promotion, or even change in title. Their bosses provide excuses like:

• "We have budget constraints."
• "This is a great opportunity to prove yourself."
• "We'll revisit it in a few months to see how you do."

While the long-term efficacy of this approach is questionable, it doesn't appear to be going away anytime soon. If you find yourself in a similar situation, you must figure out two things.

How to deal with it in the short term to maintain your sanity and how to leverage it in the long term for advancement in tangible terms. After all, if you're given this "opportunity," you're not doing it for the privilege of even more work and no rewards.

## STOP IS A SHORT-TERM FIX

When the "opportunity" is piled on to existing responsibilities, it can result in increased stress and uncertainty. Your immediate concern needs to be recognizing and managing your stress level. When dealing with stress, alternative medicine proponent Dr. Deepak Chopra recommends the STOP approach:[29]

- **S: Stop** what you are doing.
- **T: Take** a few deep breaths.
- **O: Observe** the sensations in your body and smile.
- **P: Proceed** with awareness and compassion.

Chopra also recommends meditation, which can help to keep your mind and body connected and provide critical perspective on your situation. I recommend that you try not to lose sight of what's reasonable.

In my own situation, I continually reminded myself that I was doing the work that two people had done previously. I realized I had to adjust my own expectations about what could be done in the number of hours I was willing to devote to this job and to focus on the top priorities for each role.

---

29  *"Why Deepak Chopra Wants You to STOP."* SuperSoul Sunday, Oprah Winfrey Network. YouTube. https://www.youtube.com/watch?v=S-FYetaUP7Wg, Jul 1, 2012

## STAYING GROUNDED

Strangely, just acknowledging that fact to myself kept me grounded. Though I'm driven, I also recognized that I needed to set some boundaries. Working eighty hours per week for the same paycheck I'd earned working forty-five to fifty hours wasn't feasible or even possible.

Though I wasn't given a real choice to refuse the additional responsibility, I did have a choice about how I'd define what success looked like for me. I spent a lot of time reminding my boss about what was reasonable and the extraordinary lengths that I was going to in managing these two roles. I didn't want my two jobs for one paycheck to become the new normal.

It's critical to maintain a healthy perspective so you don't get so caught up in the unrelenting demands of work that you aren't enjoying your life and finding ways to refill your energy supplies. Remember, there's more to life than your job.

## PLAY THE GAME FOR WHAT YOU'RE WORTH

Similar to taking on a lot more for the same pay, it's not uncommon for people to be asked to do more work with no additional pay when special circumstances arise like the departure or illness of a coworker, a big project with a looming deadline, or other special situations.

Managing your stress level when you're asked to take on significantly more responsibility for the same pay is important. Maintaining your energy is the priority when you're faced with this situation, closely followed by keeping a healthy perspective.

We've been conditioned to expect more pay when we're asked to undertake more responsibilities. I'll share some strategies for how to use the experience to get ahead in the long term.

## IS IT TEMPORARY OR PERMANENT?

First, I want to be clear on what I'm talking about . . . I'm not talking about being asked to stay late for a few days or even weeks as your organization works toward a critical deadline. That type of situation, while tiring and potentially frustrating, is temporary with a foreseeable end date. That's really part of business as usual.

What I'm referring to is when you're asked to take on significantly more responsibility with no promise of additional compensation or a promotion and with no foreseeable end date. These situations typically arise when team members leave and their roles are either filled slowly or not at all, but the work does not stop or slow down. Or perhaps a supervisor leaves and her second-in-command is expected to step in and fill the former boss's shoes but without the boss's title, compensation, or clout. (This is essentially the situation I experienced and described earlier in this chapter.)

This can happen when management:

- Has difficulty finding a suitable replacement,
- Is too busy to recruit,

- Anticipates a restructuring that would make the former role obsolete,
- Takes advantage of cost savings while not paying the departed employee's salary, or
- Doesn't understand the impact of not filling the role more quickly.

If you are one of the employees expected to take up the slack, it can sometimes be hard to maintain a positive outlook. You are working harder and may feel like no one notices, which often results in feelings of helplessness and resentment. In these situations, recognize your own value even if you feel like others are not.

### LEVERAGE THE NEW SITUATION

Though feelings of frustration or anger in these situations are perfectly understandable, do whatever you can to maintain a positive attitude, because, bottom line, opportunity is opportunity.

*"The Chinese use two brush strokes to write the word 'crisis.'*
*One brush stroke stands for danger,*
*the other for opportunity."*

— JOHN F. KENNEDY[30]

---

30  Kennedy, John F. Remarks at the Convocation of the United Negro College Fund, Indianapolis, Indiana, April 12, 1959. https://www.jfklibrary.

When rapid change takes place, by being savvy, you can ride it to a better place and benefit from the change. Be clear about how you can leverage the new situation to get something that you want out of it.

## WHAT DO YOU WANT?

First, give some thought to what you want. It's often harder than it sounds to know what you really want . . . Consider these things:

- Do you like what you've been asked to do?
- Is this something that you'd like to do long term?
- If the answer is yes, what else would you like to go along with the additional responsibility? More money? An elevated title? More resources?
- Get clear on your desired outcome, then approach your boss and let him know what you want and ask about what you need to do to make it happen.

One of three things could happen:

1. You could be given what you ask for or be told it's something that will be seriously considered.

2. You could be told the conditions under which you'll be granted your request.

---

org/archives/other-resources/john-f-kennedy-speeches/indianapo-lis-in-19590412. Accessed January 25, 2020.

3. You could be told you cannot have what you want for a variety of reasons that could range from no budget, lack of willingness to go to bat for you, or (ironically) not seeing you as qualified for the role or promotion (though you may already be doing the job by default!).

## LEVERAGING THE OPPORTUNITY

Each of these answers gives you information you can use in determining your next step.

- If you get what you ask for, congrats! Now get clear on the expectations and deliver.

- If you are given clarity on the steps to earn the promotion and/or a raise, that's good news! You have clarity and can start developing a plan to get what you want.

- Once you've implemented your plan and met the conditions that were communicated, make your boss aware of it and ask her to follow through on the commitment she made. If she does, congrats! If she doesn't, then by default, you're at the final option.

- If you are asked to take on significantly more responsibility on a permanent basis for the same rewards, you will have some decisions to make. You've already thought about what you want, you've asked for it, and you've been told your request won't be fulfilled. So now what?

## GETTING WHAT YOU WANT ... ELSEWHERE

Use your experience to get what you want . . . at a different firm. List your additional responsibilities and results on your résumé and LinkedIn profile. Also, use a title that is descriptive of what you do, even if it's not your actual job or title.

For example, if your boss left and all his responsibilities have been given to you, list yourself as an interim or acting director or manager of your department. If you don't feel comfortable using that as a title, you can list it in the body of your résumé in a bullet.

For instance, "After previous manager left, I served as interim department director leading team planning efforts and representing the department at the senior leadership meetings."

## TRACK YOUR ACCOMPLISHMENTS

Though you may be crazy busy, make the time to keep track of all your accomplishments. If, due to your additional responsibilities you have new access to senior leaders in the organization, take the opportunity to introduce yourself. If you have access to people from other areas of the company, use this time to build relationships.

This is called leveraging your opportunities for future gain. Through exposure to these new coworkers, you may discover new opportunities that come with additional pay, and you're placing yourself in a position where others can see your potential.

In addition to looking at positions within your own company, look outside as well. You may find your skills and experience are valued more by other organizations than your current one. In fact, that dynamic played out for me when I didn't get my boss's old job and received offers from two other companies. If you need help strategizing or brushing up on interview skills, you can read books on the topic, peruse resources on LinkedIn and YouTube, or hire a coach to help you.

## MIND YOUR IMAGE

From a wardrobe and grooming standpoint, make sure your professional image aligns with what people expect at the level you're aspiring to move up to. If you need to, invest in a haircut or an upgraded wardrobe to be perceived as a next-level leader. If you get a big raise and promotion, an investment of a few hundred dollars spent on your image will provide a big return.

## GET NON-SALARY REWARDS

Even if you don't want to leave your organization and aren't able to negotiate for a raise and/or promotion, consider asking for other forms of compensation. Managers don't always have the flexibility to grant raises or promotions but may be willing to provide other forms of value at their disposal. Here are a few ideas of what you can ask for:

- A spot in an executive or specialized training class.
- Extra vacation days.
- Tuition reimbursement.
- A better office or workstation.
- Business travel.

- Nomination for a company award.
- Membership dues for an industry association.
- A car allowance.
- Sports tickets in the company box.
- Attendance at an industry conference.

## ADVOCATING FOR YOURSELF

If you're asked to go above and beyond, make sure you come out better off for it. Remind yourself—and your boss—of the value you've brought. Be a strong advocate for yourself and the advancement of your career. With the right attitude and career management strategy, you might be the first to raise your hand the next time a big disruption happens at work because you know how to leverage it for your advancement.

## STOP HIDING YOUR BRILLIANCE

I was a freshly-minted MBA sitting in a meeting at my new employer. The issue at hand is now hazy in my memory, but what stood out to me was that everyone in the room seemed puzzled by how to approach the issue we'd encountered.

I had an idea, but I was convinced it wasn't worth mentioning because it seemed so obvious. I thought surely it had occurred to, and been rejected by, all the esteemed leaders in the room. A lively discussion went on for forty-five minutes or so when finally, the head of the group proposed an idea and immediately everyone got in line behind it. And wouldn't you know . . . it was the same idea I'd had ten minutes into the meeting and kept to myself.

Even though I'd had the idea first, because I hadn't shared it, I would not get credit or be recognized for my strategic thinking. That hurt, because I longed to make an impact and move up. I was hiding my light under the proverbial bushel. In addition, because I was too shy to speak up, many man-hours of valuable executive time were wasted. Had I shared the idea when it occurred to me, we could have fast-forwarded to discussing how to implement the idea.

## GETTING BEYOND SELF-EDITING

I'm not unique in this habit of self-editing, and I wish I could say that was the only time it happened in my career. Smart people commonly refrain from sharing ideas for fear of not being "good enough," when in fact, the idea is a good one. Maybe you've also self-edited to your own detriment.

This phenomenon begs two questions:

- What gets in the way of speaking up and sharing your ideas?

- More importantly, how can you overcome the barriers to participating fully and confidently at work so you are adding value and feeling fulfilled?

Several reasons might cause you to refrain from sharing your ideas. Each of these reasons boil down to fear—fear of negative outcomes like criticism, embarrassment, or exposure. You may also avoid speaking up because of underlying fears related to potential positive outcomes such as setting the bar for higher performance expectations or feeling pressure to execute the ideas you have come up with.

## THE RISK OF SAYING SOMETHING STUPID

Though I'm trying to provide some reassurances that sharing your ideas can garner positive results, for many, the drive to avoid a massive faux pas is just too strong to overcome. Some people fear that even one misplaced comment or impractical idea will hurt them. If this sounds like you, I suggest you start small by giving yourself goals about how much you'll speak up in meetings.

Once you've become comfortable speaking more, start sharing your ideas. If your idea gets shot down once or twice, don't fret. If you notice a pattern, ask for feedback on how you can be more effective. Your ideas may not be landing due to any number of factors—from bad timing to misunderstanding the underlying issue to the way you're communicating. Get some input to confirm you're being perceived the way you think you are.

## LET YOUR LIGHT SHINE

The key to snuffing out these fears is to get to the heart of beliefs that underpin the blocks. You could have a gremlin message wrongly telling you that you're not as good as the others in the room. Especially if you're less experienced, you might understandably put leaders on a pedestal and expect them to know more—that's not unusual.

But remember that leaders are only human and didn't start out at the top of the ladder. Usually they got there by distinguishing themselves, and if you want to get ahead, you need to do the same by showing what you know and what you can do.

You were hired to bring your ideas, experience, and unique insights to your organization. If you're invited to a meeting, you can believe that your ideas are expected and hopefully will be valued. If you have an ambition to advance in your organization, share your ideas. You make progress and show others what you're capable of only by taking risks.

# COLETTE: A VARIED AND WINDING CAREER PATH

---

Colette Aaron[31] is the director of operations for a custom home builder and also has her own construction business on the side. During a thirty-year career, she has gotten married and divorced, raised five children, and held jobs that run the gamut from waitress to TV production coordinator to construction company executive to entrepreneur. She's thrived in roles where she could use her strong skills in relationship management, creativity, and organization.

Colette's story is one of persistence. She overcame difficult challenges while being a stabilizing force in the lives of her children. Over time, she more clearly recognized her value to the organizations where she worked and stepped more

---

31  Name has been changed to protect her privacy.

fully into her power. I find her story inspiring, as she persevered through hardships that often devastate otherwise strong people.

## IN HER OWN WORDS

I'd always thought I would go into a creative field. When I went to college, I started out as a graphic design major. After a couple semesters, the work required for that major was proving much more demanding than I was prepared for. I had taken some interesting political science courses, so I decided to change my major to political science and international relations. My plan was to go to law school, but before I started applying, I realized quickly that I didn't want to be a lawyer.

## GETTING INTO (AND OUT OF) THE CORPORATE WORLD

I got out of school in the early 1990s, and the job market wasn't great. People had begun specializing a lot more in college, and here I was with this liberal arts degree. I went to work for an accounting firm, thinking I'd come in at the entry-level and work my way up.

The firm was doing the accounting for one of the biggest class-action lawsuits in the country's history. When I interviewed, it seemed like it might be interesting and even a little glamorous. Take my word for it: it wasn't. I ended up making copies all day—for thousands of cases—for about six months. It was mind-numbing, so I quit and got a job waiting tables at a steak house.

## QUADRUPLING MY INCOME

I worked a week at that steak house to earn what I made in a month at the accounting firm. I had more freedom in my life. I went to work at five or six o'clock each night and had my days to myself. It was a decent living for a twenty-something.

When I had my first child, I was able to keep working. I'd stay home with her during the day and my husband would watch her at night while I worked. I stopped working when my husband, James, started a construction company and we had our second child. At first, I wasn't that involved in his business, but as it got bigger, I started doing back-office work.

## MY FIRST FORAY INTO CONSTRUCTION

As I typed contracts and proposals for James's projects, I learned about construction almost organically. I began to understand the scope and different aspects of the business through conversations about his jobs.

After we moved back to the resort area where I grew up, I got a job at an upscale restaurant waiting tables at night during the tourist season. I was able to be home with the kids during the day and work at night to help earn money for our growing family.

## BEING PART OF A WORK FAMILY

The restaurant was a landmark institution and pretty laid-back. I felt like I was part of a family rather than an employee. My coworkers and I had close camaraderie in a high-stress situation every night, serving customers in close quarters.

The owners treated the staff like valued partners, and most of the regular clientele treated you like friends. Going home with cash tips every night provided immediate gratification. Each night, after the staff had been running around for six or seven hours, we'd all sit at the bar, relax, and have a drink together after closing. In this supportive atmosphere, I could just be myself.

The restaurant was actually a nice, creative environment in an old funky building. We displayed artwork from local artists, so the restaurant was basically also an art gallery. The owners were open to suggestions, too. The bathroom was dilapidated and not in keeping with the creativity of the rest of the place. I saw it as a blank canvas that needed something, and I had an idea for what would liven it up. The owners were like, "Knock yourself out," so I painted a colorful mural. It felt good to be able to express myself and be appreciated for that.

### BECOMING AN ENTREPRENEUR

Over the five years I worked there, I became friends with the chef, Gayle. We both had young children and started talking about our mutual desire to do something more for our families. We came up with the idea of a catering company. Gayle had the real culinary expertise, and I focused on sales, marketing, and party planning.

We brought our kids to work during the days, then they would stay with their dads at night when we catered the parties. We did that for about four years. When a retail site opened up, we flirted with starting a gourmet grocer, but I could see the writing on the wall.

## TWO BIG LIFE TRANSITIONS

My marriage was headed for divorce, and I needed to be able to support my family in a bigger way. Gayle didn't want to do the store, so at that point, we decided to amicably part ways from a business standpoint.

I went back to school to study architectural engineering. Custom homes were in high demand in the resort area where I lived. I had some experience in construction from helping with James's business. From a creative aspect, I thought it would be a good fit for me.

It was tough getting through the two-year program while I was going through a divorce and raising five kids—the youngest was a toddler. The economy didn't help either. When I started in 2007, the program had a ninety-eight percent placement rate for graduates. I graduated in 2009 during the financial meltdown when the housing market was terrible, so demand for my degree tanked to zero at that time.

## A TIGHT JOB MARKET

I just needed to get a job to support myself and my kids, and I began applying for roles beyond construction. Then, I noticed a new builder was renovating office space near where I lived. One day, I stopped by their office unsolicited, introduced myself, and dropped off my résumé.

A few days later, they called me in for an interview. I don't think they knew what they even needed until they saw my résumé. They said, "We weren't even looking for anyone, but when we saw your skill set, we realized this might be something that we need."

## THE PERFECT FIT

I was so excited. I felt lucky to get up every day and go to work there. I started out part time—only about thirty hours per week as sort of an administrative assistant. At such a small company that was growing rapidly, I just stepped into anything that needed to be done. Eventually the office manager left, so it was just me and the two partners in the office.

I kept moving up. First, I was the project coordinator dealing with clients as we moved through all the creative stages of designing and building their custom homes—the house design, then interior design. As the company grew, I was promoted to the role of vice president of sales and marketing, and I had people working under me.

## A PUNCH IN THE GUT

I worked there for about five years. I remember at one point, one of the partners said,

> *"Who knew what Colette was really capable of*
> *when we hired her?*
> *Who knew she could do all the things*
> *she's done for this company?"*

Honestly, I was a little offended. I thought, "Well, I always knew I could do it." It made me wonder what they'd thought of me. They certainly weren't seeing me as I saw myself.

Though I'd been there from the beginning and helped grow the business, as time went on, I started to see some troubling signs I had wanted to ignore. The first sign was when they decided to hire a guy as vice president of operations who had previously run his own construction company.

One of the partners checked in to make sure I was okay with them hiring him.

I was like, "Yeah, why wouldn't I be?"

He said, "Well, he's going to be your boss."

That news was like a punch in the gut.

I'd been with them from the beginning and had done whatever needed to be done. I'd made order out of the chaos by developing processes and procedures that the business needed, and I was the day-to-day contact with our clients. I'd even met and recommended a consultant to help them figure out how to scale the company, and this was how they were going to thank me?

## ME AND A BUNCH OF MEN

I wasn't happy reporting to the new vice president of operations, but I thought I'd keep an open mind and see how it went. I thought maybe I'd learn something from the new guy, but that wasn't to be. That hire started a period of company expansion.

As the owners pursued their vision, they hired all men, except for the female receptionist, and brought all the new hires on at either my level or higher. I later found out that a man who was hired much later at my same level was making twenty-four thousand more than me. I found it hard not to see this as a case of gender discrimination.

A pattern started to emerge. The partners stated that they wanted my role to be narrower and more well-defined, but even guys in the field were coming to me for direction because I knew what was going on. A few years after the company's founding, one of the partners left the business.

During that critical transition, I worked seven days a week for eight weeks to make sure all our projects moved ahead according to plan. If I didn't provide direction, mistakes would be made, and I'd end up having to fix them.

### MY VALUE WASN'T RECOGNIZED

The company's revenue quadrupled in the time I was there. I don't think about my gender—I am just a person who is focused on doing whatever needs to be done. Though I played a pivotal role in the firm's success and though I didn't want to acknowledge bias against me, it became shockingly clear that I wasn't being fairly compensated based on my contributions to the firm.

### A NEW CHALLENGE: TELEVISION AND CONSTRUCTION

About the time that I was considering leaving, I was approached by a builder who had gotten a TV show on the DIY network. She wanted me to join her team as a production coordinator to serve as the liaison between the TV production company in New York and her construction company.

I've watched a lot of those home shows on the HGTV and DIY networks. Knowing so much about the building industry, I was curious to see how these shows really worked. I worked with the production company and film crew when they came down from New York for filming.

I was on-site and communicating with the director between shooting days to make sure we were getting input from the designers they hired to do the home and interior designs. The projects were fast-moving because we had to complete them on schedule to correspond with the broadcast dates.

I found it really interesting. At the end of the year, the show wrapped up and I moved on. I enjoyed it for a while, but the pace of TV ultimately isn't well aligned with construction.

**IF THEY CAN DO IT, I CAN DO IT!**
I had learned a lot about construction over the years as I worked for other people. I figured if they could do it, I could do it, so I decided to start my own construction company. About the same time, another custom builder contacted me about helping him manage the kickoff of a development he was breaking ground on. He was busy running the other parts of his business, and this project needed focused, hands-on management.

I took the job with the agreement that I would continue doing projects on my own in the evenings and on weekends. I began that job and also managed renovations and new construction builds through my own company.

It's been about twenty years since I was first exposed to the construction industry by helping my ex-husband with his business. Now, I'm the director of operations for a custom home builder that builds multimillion-dollar homes, and I'm running my own construction company on the side. It's a little mind-blowing. I never would have foreseen this in college when I was weighing the pros and cons of graphic design and law.

### AT A CROSSROAD

Now, I'm at a crossroad. One of the things that has driven me a little crazy over the years is working for companies that don't have good organization and processes. I like efficiency and seeing things moving along as they should. It took me a while to recognize that organization and process engineering are strengths of mine.

It bothers me to have to redo things or have delays that could be avoided by implementing and following a well-thought-out process. It's one of the biggest issues I have with my job right now.

I end up having to fix things because my employer resists instituting more consistent processes within the organization. The owner seems satisfied to work the way he always has. He's been successful to this point, so it's certainly his prerogative.

If I worked in my own company, I would have control and wouldn't need to continually present to others the benefits of consistent processes leading to efficiency, and ultimately, higher profitability.

## AT A CRITICAL DECISION POINT

I need to make the decision between staying with the security of a full-time job with decent compensation or leaving to do my own thing so I can have more control. Do I go for it and dedicate all my time to my business? Or do I try to straddle the fence—as I am right now—between a secure full-time job and juggling my part-time business?

A key factor for my future success is finding reliable subcontractors to work with me. It's a bit of a chicken-and-egg problem—the reliable subs want reliable work, and I can't provide that to them if I only do this part time. But in order to go full time, I'll need reliable subcontractors. At some point, I need to take a leap of faith.

## EXERCISE: IDENTIFYING WHAT HOLDS YOU BACK

Spend some time journaling on these questions:

- If you're not satisfied with your current job situation, what stands in the way of making a change?
- How able are you to ask for what you want?
- How clear are you on how you add value to your organization?
- Do those above you recognize the value you bring? If not, how can you communicate it to them clearly?
- If you are undervalued, what will you do about it? Could other organizations value you more than your current organization?
- Are you stepping fully into the power you have, meaning that you use it freely and without asking permission? If not, why not?
- What skill gaps do you have that would help you be more effective if you mastered them?
- Where is "good enough" getting in the way of achieving greatness?
- What would you need to take the leap toward what you really want to do?

## CHAPTER 9

# AT THE TOP OF YOUR GAME: Tips And Tools For Staying Productive

———

*Give me a place to stand, and with a
lever I will move the whole world.*

−ARCHIMEDES[32]

When I began working with Leigh, she had a leverage problem. She'd recently been promoted from the manager of a team of eight to the director of a department of fifty. Her pride of having worked her way up from individual contributor over ten years was interwoven with her anxiety about fulfilling the responsibilities entrusted to her.

---

32  Tzetzes, John. Book of Histories (Chiliades) 2. Translated by Francis R. Walton. p. 129-130.

## WORKING ALL THE TIME

In our first session, she shared that she was working ten to twelve hours each weekday and taking work home with her on the weekends. As the mother of young children, she was frustrated that she was working up to seventy hours a week, but she rarely saw her team putting in extra hours.

She was driven to succeed in her new position but also recognized that the pace she'd set for herself was not sustainable. She hoped we could develop some strategies that would allow her to reduce her work hours and feel more in control of her department.

After getting a better understanding of Leigh's situation, I recognized a pattern that is common with many newly-promoted leaders. Though she'd moved up a level in the organization, she was still operating in the same way she had when she was a first-line manager. This approach was costing her a lot in terms of her own time, energy, and peace of mind.

## SOLVING THE LEVERAGE PROBLEM

In its simplest form, leverage is defined as gaining an advantage through the use of a tool. Leigh was not using the tools at her disposal as a department leader to make her work easier. It was as if she had a wheelbarrow at her disposal but instead decided to carry a load of bricks one-by-one to the jobsite.

The solution to her leverage problem was two-pronged. The first prong pertained to her mindset and her ability to gain a level of comfort with her new position and the power that came along with it. In other words, she needed to accept that the wheelbarrow was hers to use.

The second prong—which I'll address in the remainder of this chapter—was developing processes for how to best stack the bricks in the wheelbarrow to efficiently complete the job.

Here are some of the specific areas we worked on to help her gain leverage:

- Prioritization
- Goal Setting
- Delegation
- Time Management
- Focus

### UNDERSTANDING WHAT'S EXPECTED

In Leigh's case, she was clear on what she needed to do. She had joined the company as an individual contributor in the department she now led. She knew how to do the jobs of nearly everyone in the department and, in some ways, that was a hindrance to her. When she'd been a manager, she functioned as a player *and* coach.

She had other individual contributors reporting to her, and she also had projects of her own to manage. If anyone on her team stumbled or didn't deliver as expected, Leigh could jump in and get the project back on track.

This successful strategy led to her promotion. However, because she knew how to do the day-to-day work so well, it wasn't critical for her to learn how to direct and lead her staff more efficiently.

## A BIGGER JOB REQUIRES A NEW APPROACH

When she was promoted, while she understood the expectations, she did not feel comfortable taking a more hands-off approach to leading. Rather than allowing her staff to struggle with challenges and build their capabilities, she had trained them to come to her to rescue them from problems.

This, in turn, caused the problem she struggled with—there simply was not enough of her to go around. She couldn't troubleshoot the work of fifty people as she'd been able to do when she managed only eight.

## STOP BABYING AND START DELEGATING

Here's an analogy to better illustrate. When toddlers first learn to use a spoon, they make a mess every time. As a parent, it can be tempting to just feed them yourself. But without allowing the child to try it on their own, a parent might still be spoon-feeding a twelve-year-old.

Would that make sense? Of course not! Cleaning pureed carrots out of a tot's hair is the short-term price parents pay for the freedom of not having to hand-feed their child for the next seventy years.

Obviously, this is a little bit of an exaggeration, but you get the point. Letting go of the control for the greater good is the same lesson Leigh had to learn.

## FIRST THINGS FIRST

The first step in developing Leigh's roadmap to working a reasonable schedule started by determining her priorities. This isn't always easy, because we sometimes confuse urgency with importance. In Leigh's situation, this was the case.

She complained that, because of her open-door policy, she was so busy solving her staff's problems that she never had time during the day to complete her own work. This led her to work a lot of hours on weekends when she would rather be with her husband and kids.

As we worked together, we used the Eisenhower Box[33] as our guide. This tool was developed by President Dwight D. Eisenhower and popularized in Stephen Covey's best-seller *The 7 Habits of Highly Effective People*.[34] It is a four-box matrix with importance on one axis and urgency on the other to help prioritize activities.

Important and urgent things get highest priority. These may include crises and project deadlines. Activities that are important but not urgent are often not prioritized as highly as they should be.

---

33 "Introducing the Eisenhower Matrix." https://www.eisenhower.me/eisenhower-matrix/. Accessed February 1, 2020.

34 Covey, Stephen R. The 7 Habits of Highly Effective People: Powerful Lessons in Personal Change. Simon & Schuster, 1989. p. 151.

hat it looks like:

| | |
|---|---|
| **Important but not urgent** SCHEDULE WHEN YOU WILL DO IT | **Urgent and important** DO IT IMMEDIATELY |
| **Not important and not urgent** DO LATER OR DON'T DO | **Urgent but not important** DELEGATE TO SOMEBODY ELSE |

IMPORTANCE

URGENCY ────────────────────▶

## URGENT VERSUS IMPORTANT

In Leigh's case, that was certainly true. With her open-door policy, she ended up working on more urgent but not important activities such answering her staff's questions, and this distracted her from the important but not urgent activities such as staff training, relationship building, evaluating opportunities, planning, and troubleshooting.

> *"What is important is seldom urgent and what is urgent is seldom important."*
>
> —DWIGHT D. EISENHOWER[35]

---

35  "How to be More Productive and Eliminate Time Wasting Activities by Using the 'Eisenhower Box'" https://jamesclear.com/eisenhower-box. Accessed February 1, 2020.

## DETERMINING PRIORITIES

I asked Leigh to go through a five-step process to examine how she spent her time at work. Here are the steps we took that changed her life and hopefully will do the same for you:

- **Inventory tasks.** Make a list of all tasks you need to complete on a daily, weekly, monthly, quarterly, and annual basis.
  - Rank by importance. Rank the tasks in terms of the importance to your mission.
    - The first-level priority would be "extremely critical," meaning the business would shut down or be significantly impacted if these tasks weren't done on time.
    - Second-level priorities are critical and could rise to first level if not addressed soon.
    - Third-level priorities are important but will not put anything at immediate risk if not done in the short term. These can wait until you have more discretionary time.
    - The lowest-ranking priorities are nice to have, meaning the business could continue on with little-to-no disruption if these tasks aren't done. Sometimes, we may prefer to do the nice-to-have activities, but you must make sure you're not prioritizing these activities over higher-level priorities.
    - Look to eliminate tasks that are obsolete or add no value. Sometimes, processes are not updated to reflect changes in the business. When in doubt, ask if these activities add any value and eliminate those that don't.

- **Match tasks to skill sets.** Take yourself as a manager out of the equation and honestly evaluate your employees' skills. Review the tasks to determine which require your direct involvement and which can be done by someone else.
  - Are you the best person to be doing this task? If you don't absolutely *have* to do it, train someone else to do it and delegate.
  - How much overlap is there between what you and others do within the organization?
  - Could one of the processes be tweaked so the other could be eliminated? Use the "hit by a bus" rule to determine how the task would be done if you could not complete it—meaning how would this task be done if you were hit by a bus and couldn't perform? If an alternative way to complete the task is available, challenge yourself to implement that solution now to free up more of your time and focus.
  - True, you may be better at each task than anyone on your team, but don't fall into the trap of doing a task because you can do it faster. Find the person who can do it second best and delegate! Reserve your time for your highest-value work and delegate everything else.
- **Triage tasks based on time needed to complete.** After ranking the tasks, look at the tasks at each level of importance and determine which can be done quickly and which require more time, effort, and focus.
  - Work on the "quick hit" tasks in some cases to get them out of the way first and free up resources to work on the more complex tasks.

- Start your day with an activity that is easy to complete to give yourself a feeling of accomplishment. Sometimes that's just the encouragement you need, particularly if your next task is one that requires a longer period of effort and concentration.
- Intersperse high-priority activities with lower-level priorities that take less time to maintain energetic momentum as you go through your day.

- **Align expectations.** As you go through this process, you may discover insights you need to share with others in your organization—superiors, peers, clients, and vendors. Use your insights to ensure your goals are aligned with the expectations of those around you. You may discover additional changes are needed to the structure, processes, or people in your organization.
- **Calendar your activities.** Things that get scheduled get done. It's as simple as that.

### SETTING SMART GOALS

Goals are the desired result of your efforts and are closely related to priorities; however, goals and priorities are not always the same thing. Sometimes priorities are broader, more multifaceted, and may make it hard to determine what actions to take. A useful framework that can help you develop an action plan for achieving your goals is the SMART goal process.[36]

---

36  Haughey, Duncan. "A Brief History of SMART Goals." https://www. projectsmart.co.uk/brief-history-of-smart-goals.php. December 13, 2014. Accessed January 25, 2020.

A **SMART goal** is:

- **SPECIFIC**—What do you want to accomplish? Who is responsible? What steps will be taken?
- **MEASURABLE**—How will you know it's been achieved? How will you determine success?
- **ATTAINABLE**—Is it possible given the parameters (staff, budget, current situation, etc.)?
- **RELEVANT**—Does this goal support your overall objectives?
- **TIME-BASED**—What's the final deadline? What are the interim deadlines?

Here's an example of a smart goal:

John has set a goal to be promoted from assistant vice president to vice president of the marketing department and earn a raise of at least ten-thousand dollars within the next twelve months by achieving the goals his boss has set for him.

- **SPECIFIC**—The goal is clear—a promotion from AVP to VP of marketing.
- **MEASURABLE**—The title is a yes or no decision, and the salary increase is measurable.
- **ATTAINABLE**—Yes. This goal should be attainable since John has talked with his boss

to understand what needs to be done to earn this promotion.

- **RELEVANT**—Yes. John is in marketing and wants to be promoted within that department. Had the goal been to be promoted to VP of accounting, it would not be relevant.
- **TIME-BASED**—Yes. A date has been determined—this time next year.

## PARSING YOUR GOALS INTO META-GOALS

If your goal is large, it may be helpful to break your goal down into smaller, more achievable SMART goals so you can make progress and keep up your momentum with a sense of accomplishment.

In this case, John might develop a series of supporting SMART goals for various aspects of the larger goal that his boss set for him as a condition for promotion. They might include completing training, fulfilling project deadlines, or gaining more exposure within the organization.

## EXPLORE OPTIONS

Sometimes we don't know what we don't know. We may recognize that our current situation isn't working, but we're not sure how to change it. Or perhaps we know what the final outcome needs to look like but have no idea how to get started. Don't feel ashamed for not knowing something. People have either done the exact thing you're trying to do or at least have done something similar.

## GET CURIOUS

Start talking to people who know something about the goal you're trying to achieve. Who has done it before? Where can you find articles, podcasts, or books on the topic? Don't let your fear or shyness hold you back from learning from people who have been there, are there now, or are a few steps ahead of you on the journey.

Though we may sometimes fear rejection, most people really like to talk about their passions, as well as their successes and how they got there. Talk to people in your company, in clubs or associations to which you belong, alumni groups, or vendors.

## WHO KNOWS WHO?

Look for people in your network who know the people you want to talk with and ask for an introduction. If you don't have those contacts, reach out cold and ask for a quick phone call or offer to buy coffee. Search on LinkedIn by job title or company. Send messages through their websites if you can't find an email address. When you connect, express genuine interest in what they are doing.

Recognize that some of the experts you're reaching out to may be busy, so they may not say yes or may have limited time. If they don't respond or can't meet with you, it's not about you. Just move on to the next person on your list.

When you do make contact, be respectful of their time and patience and always say thank you!

## DON'T GET STUCK HERE

A word of warning—it can be easy to get stuck at this step with analysis paralysis. You may be tempted to look for the perfect path forward or want to talk to just one more person in hope that they will have the ideal advice for you.

At some point, if you want to make progress toward your goal, you'll need to take action. It may be the right action and it might not, but you will learn and be able to make a better choice with your next step. Just try something and see how it goes.

## COMMIT TO YOUR GOAL

Once you've decided what you want to do and developed a plan to achieve it, you must commit to it. Write it down. Tell other people. Do whatever you must to ensure you remain focused on completing your goal.

Being accountable to other people is an important key to success in meeting your goals. Ask someone to be your accountability buddy and provide updates to them as you move toward your goal. As humans, we're more likely to take action if we know someone else expects it than if we're only accountable to ourselves.

One caveat about commitment . . . if circumstances change, you are allowed to revise your goal along the way. Often, you may think a particular outcome is what you need, but as you progress toward it, you may learn that another solution may be better.

It's absolutely okay to pivot to something different without feeling guilty or like you've failed. Just make sure you're not wimping out when it gets hard. You may be tired and frustrated at times, and when that happens, give yourself a temporary break. Catch your breath and regain your focus. After you've taken your break, get back on the path to your goal.

## CONNECT AND BUILD ALLIANCES

When you're pursuing a goal, whether personal or professional, it can sometimes feel lonely. Finding fellow travelers who know what you're going through can help keep you focused. If you could use support as you're pursuing your goal—particularly if the goal is dependent on others, such as finding a new job—building your network could be an important part of achieving it.

Consider whether collaborating with others in your organization or putting together your own tribe of supporters could be helpful. If so, go to networking events or clubs that are focused on the thing you want to do. Look for specialized social media networking groups on LinkedIn, Facebook, Instagram, and other platforms. Engage in these groups.

It's amazing how well you can get to know people online even if you never meet in person. The exchange of ideas can be energizing and encouraging. If you find someone you would like to get better connected with, ask them if they'd be willing to do a virtual coffee by videoconference or phone.

When you reach out to people, you can build rapport by letting them know what caught your attention—for example, if you have mutual contacts, if you work in the same industry, or if they posted a comment that resonated with you, let them know!

## COFFEE CAN PAY DIVIDENDS

Leigh recognized she needed to build her network to achieve her goal of raising her leadership profile within her organization. She began by making a list of the people with whom she'd like to build closer relationships. She already knew some key partners on her list and she simply needed to be more intentional about nurturing those relationships.

In other cases, she requested others introduce her people she needed to meet. She began to tack an additional day onto trips to her company's headquarters, and she made advance plans to meet with her colleagues for coffee, lunches, dinners, and drinks during her free time while on business trips.

She gained a deeper understanding of the dynamics within the organization as she had conversations with colleagues in other offices. Over time, she was more comfortable going to the quarterly strategy meetings off-site because she knew more people.

She also found that she was getting more calls asking for her input on various topics simply because colleagues knew her better and understood her area of expertise and how she could help them.

## GETTING SUPPORT

Accountability is key in achieving goals. To make progress, take action. Leigh committed to specific actions in support of her goals at the end of each coaching session. At the start of the next session, she would tell me what progress she made. Knowing she had to provide an update to me was an incentive to take action.

When she didn't take action, we talked about that as well. Sometimes, she had mental blocks or fears that stood in the way. We would discuss them with the intention of shifting her mindset to a more action-oriented place.

When you're developing a roadmap to get to your goals, consider what other types of support you may need and ask for them. Examples may be increasing your delegation to your team so you can focus on the goal; requesting that a spouse, partner, or kids temporarily take on more work at home so you can focus; or asking your boss for additional training, resources, or tools. Set yourself up for success by recognizing what you'll need and asking for it.

Depending on the complexity and significance of your goal, you may consider hiring a coach or finding a buddy to help you stay on task as you move toward your goal.

## YOU'VE GOT LEVERAGE... USE IT!

If you feel overwhelmed by the demands of your job, take a big step backward so you can see the challenge clearly. Rather than using your brute strength to muscle through the tasks on your to-do list, consider your points of leverage—prioritization, goal setting, delegation, time management, and focus—and how you can use them to make your workload lighter.

If you're not sure where to start, read books such as *The 7 Habits of Highly Effective People* by Stephen R. Covey, take training classes, find a mentor, or hire a coach. Chapter 10 provides more tips for gaining leverage in your job.

# LAURA: LETTING CURIOSITY BE HER GUIDE

———

Laura Yunger is the CEO of Saltare Solutions, a management consulting firm. After more than twenty-five years in the corporate world working for huge multinational corporations as well as start-ups and small businesses, she left to start her own firm.

Laura is an explorer who let her curiosity guide her right from the beginning of her career. She learned that she never encountered a challenge she was unable to conquer. While trying to make a few bucks before going to grad school, she discovered that the fast-paced and intellectually-challenging world of finance was a surprisingly good fit for her.

Her willingness to stay open and curious netted her many opportunities throughout her career. I hope you'll take away that, sometimes, just saying yes as opportunities which present themselves is enough to advance. Laura bet she could learn the skills needed to succeed along the way, and it paid off for her again and again.

## IN HER OWN WORDS

When I started my career, I had absolutely no idea what I wanted to do. When I went to college, I was good at English, so I decided to major in journalism. I thought it would be a valuable transferable skill. When I graduated, my plan was to go to graduate school for public health nutrition. I had some health issues related to nutrition, so I had an interest in that and how it can affect the body.

### A FORAY INTO FINANCIAL SERVICES

I needed to take some prerequisite science classes to get into grad school, and while I was doing that, I took a job at a small investment company owned by a friend's father. I saw myself as this artsy journalist. I'd never thought in a million years that I'd be working in financial services, but after a while, I completely fell in love with it.

### STARTLING GROWTH AND LOTS OF OPPORTUNITY

While I was working there, the company was growing at a tremendous pace, and I had so much opportunity to do so many different things. I raised my hand for whatever seemed interesting to me. That experience framed the way I thought about my career from that time forward. I recognized early on that I was in charge of my career and had a lot of control over my own destiny because of what I was able to accomplish at that investment firm.

I was there for seven years and probably had five different roles based on what the needs of the company were at the time. As gaps or roles would arise, I'd say, "Oh, I want to do that." Each new role gave me confidence to keep challenging myself. With each new project, I stepped up and was successful. As I completed a project, I'd just move onto something new. Learning that I could jump in and figure out what needed to be done was such an important lesson to learn early in my career.

### AN IMPORTANT PIVOT POINT

I got into UC Berkeley and I was planning on leaving the firm to attend grad school. Before I left, the CEO took me aside and said,

> *"You're doing great here, and if you stay,*
> *there's a lot of opportunity for you."*

He opened my eyes to the fact that I had the option of putting off school for a year, but the opportunity in front of me at the firm might not be there later.

It was definitely a "seize the day" moment. I am so grateful for his insights. It was the early 1990s and the economy was booming. Being new in the job market, I didn't realize what a special time it was. I was getting in on the ground floor of a career with an investment company when this sector was experiencing explosive growth. I was in the right place at the right time.

## DEFERRING GRADUATE SCHOOL

I decided to defer going to graduate school, and things took off for me at the firm. After that, I never felt the need to go back to school. I had found what I liked. The investment industry was cerebral, interesting, and dynamic. And surprisingly, it was also creative.

I worked mostly in the marketing department, where I translated the technical aspects of the business into language that investors could easily understand. It was a good use of both my creative and analytical strengths. This was a good path for me.

I learned so many valuable lessons through that experience. Allow yourself to change your mind about your goals if something better presents itself along the way. Be open to opportunities, adapting as things change, and don't feel obligated to go down a certain prearranged path.

## CONNECTING SUCCESS AND HAPPINESS

I'm happy with where I've been in my career. I've always sought work I enjoyed doing. If it ever gets to the point where I'm bored, I don't like what I'm doing anymore, or I've outgrown it, I'll look for the next thing. Whether it's within the same organization or outside.

always looking for something that will challenge and e me. I've taken the responsibility on myself, and I know it's up to me to figure out what I want to do in my career. I've been able to find personal happiness for the most part, but obviously, I've had times where it's not been easy.

## TAKING CHARGE OF YOUR CAREER

You have to take charge of your career and be cognizant of making it happen. Otherwise, it can be pretty easy to just go along for the ride and do whatever you are asked to do. Kind of like being a passenger on the bus instead of being the driver. That might be fine for some people, but it definitely isn't for me.

I'm the driver. I'm always thinking about the next step. Maybe the next step is not up. It could be sideways. I'm always keeping that next goal in mind. What's the next thing I want to do? I'm not the kind of person who needs a lot of recognition. I always want to be creating something. That's the reward that I seek in my career.

## UNDERSTANDING CAREER SATISFACTION DRIVERS

In the beginning of my career, I was fortunate enough to be in an organization that was growing phenomenally well. There was so much that needed to be done, I could just jump into things that in another company I wouldn't have had the chance to do so early in my career. By the time I left after seven years, I had been able to wear many hats. It allowed me to see what was possible, what I was good at, and where I could excel naturally.

Later, I did more personal discovery—taking personality tests, hiring career and lifestyle coaches, and also joining different networking groups. Over time, I was able to understand my natural strengths more clearly. Now, I try to focus on using my strengths and not worrying about trying to do things I'm not as good at.

## COMMON PITFALLS IN FINDING CAREER SUCCESS

One of the big mistakes I've seen people make in their careers is to focus on doing things for other people in hopes that it will help them advance. In these scenarios, people can end up doing things they don't like to do and putting the power in someone else's hands. The person may be literally used without getting anything in return and then left to feel miserable. It's a losing battle to get caught up in trying to meet someone else's expectations.

## ON KNOWING YOURSELF

I'm not really sure why I had the confidence to transcend worrying about what other people thought of my career choices. I just know I have to enjoy what I'm doing. I want to be challenged and always learning. I do get bored rather easily.

My second job after college was at a huge national bank. It was an interesting contrast going there after being at the smaller firm where I was able to wear so many different hats. All of a sudden, at the big bank, I had a role where I basically had to wear blinders.

I didn't have the freedom to do what I saw needed to be done. I needed to stay in my lane so as not to step on the toes of the other specialists around me. I was supposed to work within the narrow confines of my role. To me, doing that was the easiest job in the world because it was so focused—especially after having to cover so many bases at the investment firm—but it was not necessarily the most rewarding.

## CHOOSING CHALLENGE OVER COMPENSATION

One of the great things about the big organizations is that there are a lot of opportunities for growth. At the big bank, I got a promotion to work on national accounts; after that, I moved laterally and worked on a different area of the business to help them roll out a new offering within the organization.

Had I stayed in the national accounts job, I probably would have made more money, but I took the lateral move because I knew I'd enjoy that job more. My motivation was never about getting to the top. I always want to feel like I am making a difference in any job I take.

Obviously, different people have different values. The values I hold high are being challenged and learning. Of course, compensation and recognition are important, but honestly, they are less important to me than following my passions.

## MOVING BETWEEN SMALL AND LARGE COMPANIES

I have worked at start-ups as well as some of the biggest companies in the country, and I've had success in both environments. Obviously, each has pros and cons. When I went from a smaller, family-run business to one of the largest banks in the nation, I was blown away by the resources the bank had.

With those resources, it can be easier to make a big impact. I found that a rewarding part of working at a big company. However, at large organizations, your job duties can be limited in scope. If you go outside those lines, that can be seen as a negative.

In smaller companies, you have so much more opportunity to do many things, which can be good and bad. Some people don't want to have a broad scope of responsibility and can find it overwhelming. Some people like having a specific focus and are satisfied staying within the parameters of that role. My career has not been like that.

### CAREER AGILITY

I am at heart a marketer. Some like me might only want to do marketing. For me, while that's been a big part of my career, I've also run a program management office working on finance projects and technology, I've been in sales, I've run a trading firm, and I've led strategy. I'm willing to jump into areas that seem interesting. I'm confident I'll figure out what I need to do, and I always have. I suppose confidence breeds even more confidence, and my love of learning has enabled my career agility.

I've always thought marketing professionals don't really get their just dues in terms of their ability—and requirement—to be flexible. Marketers have to hold the perspectives of the company and the customers in mind at the same time and bridge the gap to build that relationship.

### CURIOSITY, COURAGE, AND CAREER ADVANCEMENT

Relationship management and influence is critically important in your ability to succeed. I'm a curious person and I'm always open to opportunities. I found this served me well. I was willing to jump into projects where, if someone needed my help and it seemed interesting, I'd jump in. It was a "twofer"—I was helping them, and I was learning.

In my current company, which is a consulting firm, my business partner and I couldn't be more different. Sometimes, projects come our way and my partner will be doubtful about whether we can—or should—take on the project.

My attitude is always, we can do this . . . why wouldn't we and why couldn't we? Who would be better for the job? I've never felt like I couldn't do something. I've only ever asked whether I *want* to do it. I did know that I never wanted to be an accountant or a portfolio manager, so I guess that's where I'd draw the line. But I'm interested in a lot of things.

### FINDING MY OWN WAY FROM AN EARLY AGE

When I look back, I guess I have been pretty fearless in my career choices. Maybe it has something to do with my upbringing. I was the youngest of three children. My parents got divorced when I was a teenager, and I think they felt like they were basically done with parenting.

They were off doing their own things—dating and enjoying the next chapter in their lives. A little prematurely, frankly. When I was in high school, I was basically abandoned by my parents. I had to figure out my own way. A lot of bravery goes into figuring out your own way. But what would have been the alternative?

## A DRIVE TO SUCCEED

I suppose I could have just said,

> *"Okay, well, my life sucks.*
> *And I'm just gonna sit here until*
> *somebody comes along to save me."*

That was definitely not me. Something within me doesn't allow me to fail. I think that drives me a lot more than courage or bravery. I'm just going to keep pushing forward to make my visions become reality. You need to keep moving forward through your fear.

When I left my last corporate job, I looked at plenty of open positions, but most of them were roles I'd already done. Since I always want to be learning something new, those jobs were not interesting to me. That's what led me to start my own consulting company. It provides me with lots of variety and interesting challenges.

## ENTREPRENEURSHIP VERSUS BIG CORPORATE

For a few years before I started my consulting practice, I was running a small equity trading firm. I was the president and had my hands in everything that happened in the firm. Then

I got a job at a large regional bank where I headed up strategy for their wealth management business.

It was also a wide-open kind of position where I was developing and rolling out initiatives. In that role, I sometimes would see opportunities to help on initiatives in other areas of our business. I'd offer my expertise, but I'd get pushback. An attitude like, "Back off, this is my job."

### THE BOUNDARY IS DULY NOTED

I didn't take it personally though. If I was rebuffed on my offer to help, I'd just say,

## *"Okay, duly noted."*

I grew pretty thick skin, which I think goes back to the start of my career when I was working at a male-dominated financial services company. The guys I worked with did not have any filters. They were out with it, and I would not have survived if I'd taken everything personally. I was like, *Whatever*. Because, in reality, the only person's opinion I truly cared about was my own.

### CAREER CAPSTONE

Where I am now is just a natural progression from where I started. I've always liked new challenges and I'm using everything I learned throughout my career in my business now. It feels really good to know every job and every action I took before has brought me to this point and I'm using it all.

Running my own business is so fulfilling, and I don't see myself ever going back to work for someone else. If I ever did, I'd probably be okay with it as long as I was in an environment that allowed me to continue to be challenged, curious, and learning.

**EXERCISE: FOLLOWING YOUR CURIOSITY**

Spend some time thinking about and journaling your answers to these questions:

- What's your attitude toward change? Are you excited, annoyed, confused, frightened, or something else?
- When you're curious about something, do you allow yourself to follow your curiosity? If not, why?
- In what ways have you been rewarded or punished for following your curiosity? How do those experiences impact your attitude toward curiosity?
- When you follow your curiosity, what do you do? Google it? Ask people? Something else?
- How strongly do you believe things need to always be done perfectly? How has this attitude supported or thwarted your career advancement?
- What would you do if you weren't afraid? What could you do to decrease your fear?
- What do you believe will happen in your life or career if you take an action just because you want to, as opposed to feeling obligated to do something you don't want to do?

## CHAPTER 10

# LEADING A WINNING TEAM: Delegation And Other Key Leadership Skills

---

*Don't be a bottleneck . . . Force responsibility down and out. Find problem areas, add structure, and delegate. The pressure is to do the reverse. Resist it.*

—DONALD RUMSFELD, FORMER US
SECRETARY OF DEFENSE[37]

---

37   Teany, Douglas R. "Pragmatic Leadership Advice from Donald Rumsfeld."
     APPEL Knowledge Services website. https://appel.nasa.gov/2003/01/01/
     pragmatic-leadership-advice-from-donald-rumsfeld/. January 1, 2003.
     Accessed January 25, 2020.

## YOUR KEY TO PRODUCTIVITY AND SUCCESS

If you'd like to rise successfully as a leader, it's critical that you learn to delegate effectively. According to Jeffrey Pfeffer, professor of organizational behavior at Stanford University's Graduate School of Business, "Your most important task as a leader is to teach people how to think and ask the right questions so that the world doesn't go to hell if you take a day off."[38]

Unfortunately, delegation is not often taught, and sometimes the references rising leaders have are their own former managers who may not have been good role models. A 2007 study on time management conducted by the Institute for Corporate Productivity (i4cp) found that forty-six percent of the 332 companies surveyed were concerned about their employees' delegation skills. At the same time, only twenty-eight percent of those companies offered any training on the topic.[39]

## BECOME AN ALL-STAR DELEGATOR

We met Leigh in the last chapter when she'd been promoted to director and was severely overworked because she wasn't leveraging her resources wisely—including not delegating to her team.

---

38  Gallo, Amy. "Why Aren't You Delegating?" Harvard Business Review. https://hbr.org/2012/07/why-arent-you-delegating. July 26, 2012. Accessed January 25, 2020.

39  "You Want it When?" Institute for Corporate Productivity website. https://www.i4cp.com/news/2007/06/26/you-want-it-when. June 27, 2007. Accessed January 25, 2020.

I've typically seen five obstacles that hinder leaders from effective delegation. Leigh, to varying degrees, has experienced each one of these blocks. Several problems could be the cause, and once they are addressed, productivity increases. Here are the five steps to becoming a master delegator:

### 1. PROMOTE YOURSELF IN YOUR OWN MIND.

If you are caught up in the minutiae of what your staff is doing and how they are doing it rather than the impact your team is having, you are not doing your job as a leader. It might be that you are still drawn to do the work you did at a lower level. If this sounds like you, don't worry—it can be fixed.

Give yourself a promotion to leader rather than hovering around as a worker bee. Recognize your job is no longer to do that work but to ensure it gets done. Though it can feel uncomfortable at first, recognize your time is better spent on higher-level tasks. Get clear on your own objectives and then be clear with your staff about how their work needs to support it.

Paint them the big picture of what the team is working toward and how they fit into it, then step back and give them space to do their jobs. Leigh's willingness to recognize she was the leader of her department and that it wasn't up to her to solve all of the problems of her staff was a big step—and a relief—for her. It freed her to begin to focus on her own priorities and also created an environment where her staff had to solve their own problems.

Everyone likes to be part of something bigger, and as a leader, it's your job to provide that vision. When your team understands what's expected of them and they are given the freedom to deliver, you may be surprised at how fast they respond.

## 2. TRAIN YOUR STAFF.

If your staff isn't performing, it may be because you haven't spent the time to train them. In today's workplace, workers are commonly thrown into their roles and expected to wing it.

Even if that's what you experienced moving up the ranks, it doesn't mean it has to—or should—continue that way. Make a commitment to training so your team is high-performing and confident that they are delivering what's expected of them rather than struggling and slowly failing.

Provide your employees with a chance to learn their roles and to become comfortable with what's expected in a safe environment where it's okay to make a mistake. Too often, employees receive either no training at all or ineffective training. Be honest with yourself about whether you're spending too much time *doing* the work when you should be spending that time *training* your staff so *they* can do the work.

Remember the old adage, "teach a man to fish." Train your staff so you don't have to fish for them! When Leigh and I closed out our coaching engagement, she said she was proudest of the open-ended questions that she used with her staff when they came to her with problems.

By resisting the urge to jump in and solve problems, she was training her staff to come up with their own solutions and showing confidence that they were capable of achievement on their own.

In addition, make sure the proper way to perform tasks is documented and everyone is trained on the same procedures. This will reduce the time needed to train when you have staff turnover.

Once everyone has been trained and you've taken off the "training wheels," let people do their jobs without looking over their shoulders constantly. To monitor the workflow and quality, schedule periodic check-ins and let your employees tell you how they're doing rather than the other way around. That promotes ownership and excellence.

### 3. HIRE THE RIGHT PEOPLE.

If you've trained your team and you find that you still have a hard time fully delegating, it could be because you don't trust that some of your staff members are capable of performing at the expected level. If that's what's really behind your failure to step back, then you need to decide if they need more training or if any employee's skills and experience are a poor fit for the requirements for the role.

If the fit is poor, do yourself and the employee(s) a big favor and move them into roles that are a better fit or, if needed, sever the relationship. Putting off decisive action only perpetuates the problem.

I've had situations where I held on to an underperformer because I was afraid the remaining staff would be over-worked if they were to leave. What I typically found was that the staff performed better once that person had left, even before the vacant position was filled.

That told me the underperformer had a negative impact on the performance of the rest of the staff. This recognition emboldened me to be more decisive about removing under-performers more quickly after they'd been given adequate opportunities to improve and failed to do so.

### 4. TRUST YOUR EMPLOYEES.

Nobody likes a micromanager. If you don't trust your employees, ask yourself why. Has anyone on your staff shown evidence of untrustworthiness? If so, why do you continue to employ them?

If not, what is behind your lack of trust? Could it be fear on your part? People can usually sense when someone doesn't trust them and that can often be a self-fulfilling prophecy resulting in lower employee morale and motivation.

Your lack of trust could be causing a negative situation by bringing doubt into the relationship with your team and causing your employees to be self-conscious and worried, which can impact their performance. Try to create a safe environment for your employees to operate within.

Unfortunately, lack of trust in your employees could sig-nal a lack of trust in yourself. If you're setting the right expectations, hiring the right people, and training them appropriately, and still don't feel comfortable delegating, the issue might be you. Get to the root of it by doing some self-reflection or hiring a coach to help you work through it.

### 5. STAY FOCUSED ON YOUR OWN PRIORITIES.

Sometimes, it's hard to deal with the pressure of a leadership role, and rather than taking responsibility for the big picture and results, you can get caught up in the little stuff because those activities are more familiar and comfortable. The problem here is that those tasks are no longer your direct responsibility—those responsibilities rightfully belong to the people who report to you.

Being a leader can be scary because often, you're facing new challenges. You can have feelings of discomfort and even insecurity. However, that's no reason to regress, micromanage, or fail to delegate to your employees.

Take a deep breath and two giant steps back so you can get a clear view of what's really going on. If you need a confidence boost, go to your boss, mentor, or coach for help instead of driving your staff crazy by stepping on their toes and hampering their productivity.

### BE BRAVE AND LEAD

Failing to delegate is a sure way to drive good people out the door because they are not getting opportunities to grow and advance. Micromanaging can be even worse because, in effect, it tells employees the manager doesn't believe in their capability to do a good job. At the same time, the micromanager wastes his time on work that is below his pay grade and ignores the calling to be a strategic leader.

In order to continue rising within the organization, delegate so you'll be free to take on higher-level responsibilities. Step back so you can step up. Your staff will be happier and more productive, and you will enjoy more confidence and success.

### MAKING THE MOST OF YOUR TIME

You've probably been there. You come into the office in the morning with a clear set of tasks on your to-do list, but shortly after you arrive, you find yourself putting out a fire. As soon as that's done, an unexpected meeting is called where your presence is required. A phone call that you expected to last ten minutes stretches into an hour.

Each time you settle down to start on your to-do list, the little ding from the email program distracts you and you hurriedly respond to your messages. By the end of the day, you realize you'll be taking your laptop home again tonight to do the work you couldn't get done today. You think,

*"It would be nice to get my work done at work instead of always bringing it home with me."*

Your schedule running you instead of you running your schedule—a classic trap. The quandary is what to do about it. Let's solve this puzzle.

## PROTECT YOUR MOST VALUABLE RESOURCE

First, if you've done the prioritization exercise from Chapter 9, you have insights that will help you dominate your schedule instead of being dominated by it. When you clearly understand the difference between urgent and important, you are halfway to a productive solution. Be brutal when looking at how you use your time.

- Is it necessary for you to be in every meeting you're invited to?
- Can you send someone else instead?
- Can you go, give your update, and excuse yourself?
- Would it be more efficient to send a written update instead of attending and then read the meeting minutes later?

If you did the exercises in Chapter 9, you've already looked at the tasks that need to be done and sorted them into tasks you need to do yourself and those that can be delegated or stopped. With an eye to what deadlines you have coming up, look at your tasks and determine what needs to be done, how much time they need, and the type of focus they require.

For example, if you need to have uninterrupted quiet time to write, you may choose to schedule that time first thing in the morning when you are energized. Try to match the energy and focus required for the task with the time of day. Look ahead and schedule times on your calendar to work on these top priorities.

## TIME BLOCKING AND TASK BATCHING

For routine items that need to be done to keep up with workflow, such as responding to phone calls and emails, schedule a block of time to do tasks of the same sort all at once. This will allow you to get in a groove and knock them all out at the same time—and while you're at it, turn off the "you've got mail" alert on your email program. You don't need to know the moment a junk email hits your inbox. It's just robbing you of a critical resource—focus!

For example, rather than responding to emails as they come in, batching them enables you to be more efficient, especially if many of the issues you respond to may already be resolved by the time you read them. If you have any qualms about not being immediately accessible, you may want to put an "out of office" message on during your focus times to let the contact know that you'll respond at a certain time.

You can use this message or one similar to it:

> Thank you for your message. I am currently engaged in other important work, but your message is important to me. If your email requires a response, expect to hear back from me between 2:00 and 3:00 p.m. EST today. If an immediate response is needed, you may call my assistant (or other team member) at 555-555-5555.

## THE TRADE-OFFS WILL BE WORTH IT

Though at first it may be disconcerting to those who are used to hearing back from you immediately, over time they will get used to it and you'll have the satisfaction of using your time for your priorities rather than those of others. For VIPs, such as your boss, you may want to let them know your plan to block off time and provide them with alternative ways of reaching you such as your cell phone—*or not!*

You'll find that by batching similar activities together like emails, phone calls, paperwork, proofreading, or other routine tasks, you'll be more focused. You'll get much more done than if you attacked them in a haphazard way where you lose time in transition between activities.

### LEAVE SOME WIGGLE ROOM

Try not to schedule yourself too tightly. You are estimating how long tasks will take, and, despite your best efforts, sometimes things do take longer than expected. Be sure to schedule times for lunch, coffee, and bio breaks. Be sure to schedule buffers and travel time into your calendar.

If you complete the planned tasks earlier than expected, you can use the remaining time in the block to knock out some of your lower-priority work. Unless your work activities are routine on a weekly basis, you will need to block regular time to plan for each upcoming week.

You may decide to block time on Friday afternoons to look back at your prior week and adapt for the coming week based on your deliverables and what you learned. For example, are phone calls taking longer than expected? Maybe schedule a longer block. Are you finding yourself overwhelmed even with the time blocking? Perhaps more delegation or tighter prioritization is the answer.

Either way, by using this discipline on a regular basis, you'll become the master of your calendar rather than the other way around. As you get more done in less time and with less stress, you'll find you have a higher level of satisfaction with your work.

## THE POMODORO TECHNIQUE

Now that you've gone through the process of prioritizing your activities and blocking your time, you may be wondering how to focus to actually get your work done. The curiously-named Pomodoro Technique[40] is a wonderful approach to getting stuff done even when you don't have big blocks of time.

It was developed by entrepreneur and author Francesco Cirillo who named the technique for a little tomato-shaped kitchen timer he owned. (*Pomodoro* is the Italian word for tomato.)

If you're a procrastinator, as so many of us are, you know it's sometimes hard to get started on big projects or tasks. The reasons can vary—the immensity of the project may be overwhelming, you never have uninterrupted blocks of time to dedicate, or you're avoiding a task that you don't like to do. Whatever the reason, the Pomodoro Technique can help.

---

40  Henry, Alan. "Productivity 101: A Primer to the Pomodoro Technique." https://lifehacker.com/productivity-101-a-primer-to-the-pomodoro-technique-1598992730. July 12, 2019. Accessed January 25, 2020.

## HOW A POMODORO WORKS

A Pomodoro is a twenty-five-minute period of dedicated work concentrating on a single task. To start a Pomodoro, set a timer for twenty-five minutes and work exclusively on that task. You can use the timer function on your phone or set an alarm on your computer.

During this time, take no calls, don't check emails or texts, and don't take breaks—allow no distractions to interrupt your focus. When the timer goes off, take a five-minute break, and if time allows, come back after the break and do another Pomodoro.

Repeat the cycle up to four times. After you have completed four Pomodoros with five-minute breaks in between, you can take a longer break of fifteen to thirty minutes.

## THE BENEFITS OF THIS LITTLE TOMATO

The benefits of the Pomodoro Technique include:

- You can focus for twenty-five minutes, even if you don't like the task.

- When progress is made, even in small increments, you'll tend to feel more satisfied and positive about the project, thus increasing motivation to continue.

- The small periods of time between meetings or phone calls can be put to productive use if you get in the habit of doing Pomodoros during those gaps.

- For those who tend to attack projects with gusto during marathon stretches of work, forcing yourself to take breaks can actually result in increased productivity by enabling you to refresh and avoid burnout.

- Even if the marathon sessions have worked for you, they may be counterproductive, as you may find yourself avoiding starting projects because you know there will be no respite once you do.

- Shutting out distractions allows you to be productive. Even the most important phone call or email can usually wait twenty-five minutes until your break.

This technique addresses so many of the root issues causing a lack of productivity. It can be used for those routine tasks that you may not like, such as doing your expenses or filing, or it can be used for more creative work, like developing presentations or writing.

## MORE LEVERAGE MEANS MORE CONTROL

In the six months that Leigh spent incorporating these skills into her job, she experienced significantly positive results. She gained clarity on her priorities, then more effectively aligned her staff and other resources to tackle them. She began using her team for the highest-value and most important work first, thus discouraging wasted time on activities that didn't strongly support the mission of her department.

After Leigh ranked her department's tasks, she recognized that she wasn't sure if her boss shared the same view on some of the tasks that she prioritized. The exercise provided her with insights to use in a discussion with her boss and his expectations of her department. Through that, she was able to eliminate one time-consuming report that was no longer needed—a quick win!

She blocked out time on her calendar each week when she shut her door and focused on the weekly report for her boss that she had previously done over the weekend at home. She also delegated some of the activities that she'd previously completed herself to the managers on her team.

Though she'd found it easier to just do it, she recognized that, if she didn't train her staff on how to handle these situations without her, she was hobbling her department. In the case of persistent fires, she looked for patterns and developed processes to avoid or mitigate the issues that caused these distractions. Leigh encouraged her managers to go through the same process and begin to delegate or discontinue low-value work that distracted them from the more critical deliverables.

The result was that she felt more in control, was able to reduce her work hours without sacrificing output, and received feedback from her boss that she was leading her staff more effectively.

## BUILD A FOUNDATION OF SUCCESS
Use the techniques and tools discussed here in your own life. They are, in fact, as useful at home as they are at work. Whether you use them all or just one or two, these tools are

applicable in both personal and professional situations, for you, your staff, or even your family:

- Time management, including the Pomodoro Technique.
- Goal setting using SMART goals.
- Leadership skills like delegating to a team.

When you lead effectively, you'll see more positive changes take effect sooner rather than later.

# MATT:
# WORKING TO SURF

———

Matt Ryder[41] is a food scientist, surfer, and a bit of a hippie. His passion for surfing and the outdoor lifestyle was a big impetus for the career he decided to pursue even though, on the surface, it may not seem that way. He made conscious decisions to ensure these important aspects of his life complemented each other.

For whatever reason, it may not make sense to build your career around your passion. However, as Matt demonstrates in this story, if you focus on what is important to you, you may be able to build your career to accommodate that passion.

**IN HIS OWN WORDS**
I guess it started when I was in high school and in love with surfing—that idea of basically dancing on the water. As an

———

41  Name has been changed to protect his privacy.

obsessed high schooler, I was putting all my time and energy toward surfing and falling in love with it. I went to college and struggled with the question of what I wanted to do.

I ended up choosing food science as my college major primarily because the brochure for the program featured job opportunities in Indonesia and South Africa, which are both great surfing destinations. Partially because of that, I was lit up to study food science. Plus, I did like food and science—*ha ha!*

### A TIMELY EXCHANGE

Toward the end of college, I had the opportunity to go to the University of Hawaii on an exchange program. That was an all-or-nothing deal where I had to pay an application fee of around three-hundred dollars, which was a lot of money for me as a college student.

Because it was an exchange program, I was gambling that someone would want to come to Virginia Tech from the University of Hawaii. I had my doubts, but it worked out—the guy who came to Tech wanted to do the exchange because he had relatives in Virginia.

### WORKING TO SURF

The University of Hawaii had a great food science program. During the year I was in college there, I got to surf as much as I wanted. After graduation, I ended up staying and getting a job in Hawaii. I worked in a factory at night and surfed in the mornings, which was perfect. Because most people are going to work or doing other things in the mornings, it was a great opportunity to surf at those times and still work a full-time career with Frito-Lay.

## BALANCING CAREER AND PASSION

After a while, I moved to California, and Frito-Lay allowed me to choose which facility I wanted to work in. I chose Ventura Beach because the plant was only four miles away from the beach. I got to continue my daily surfing habit.

Frito-Lay is known for being the best leadership development company in the food industry, and I was gaining valuable knowledge about manufacturing processes. The job was a great fit at the time, because they spent a lot of time and energy training me to be a leader and manager of people. I did a lot of public speaking and training to lead meetings. I got experience in problem-solving and made continuous improvement. It was great.

## A COMPANY THAT SHARES MY VALUES

Now, I'm in a job at Clif Bar, and I really like the company. I knew about the company because my cousin worked there, and for fourteen years before I was hired, I had aspired to work for them. When I was working sixteen-hour days at Frito-Lay, I'd say, "Man, that company lines up with everything I value."

I was attracted to the company specifically because of their values. The benefits and time off at Clif Bar are fantastic. They are committed to being an organic company, staying employee-owned, treating employees as people, and giving them the freedom to have a family-oriented and outdoor lifestyle.

## A SHARED COMMITMENT TO ORGANIC

When I was in college, I tried to come up with an energy bar that used organic ingredients. That got me excited. For that whole time, I was looking at what Clif Bar was doing.

The company is committed to five bottom lines: business, brand, people, community, and planet. That definitely spoke to me and still does, even though sometimes I take it for granted. Their commitment to organic throughout the supply chain, from seed to shelf, is far beyond what almost any other company is doing to fund research, help out farmers, and educate people about what farmers are doing.

For a while at Clif Bar, we were assisting seed bank programs to build diverse seed populations across the country. Our commitment to serving communities and doing volunteer work is really cool. I'm excited by that. The company also has a commitment to renewable energy sources and focuses on the business's impact beyond just making a dollar.

## EXPLORING WHAT'S NEXT

But I'm wondering what to do with my career at this point. I'm forty-three, and it's pretty typical for people in their forties to wonder if they're on the right path. I want more time outside, more time in the community. I want to be surrounded by more like-minded people.

I'm in California near Berkeley, so I'm spending a lot of time with the hippies. I'd love to be out in the community, working with people on common tasks to help others. My ideas range from starting my own coaching career to living and working on a WWOOF farm. World Wide Opportunities on Organic Farms (WWOOF) is a wonderful organization that pairs advocates of organic farming with job or volunteer opportunities on organic farms to support the growth of organic foods.

### ADVICE TO MY YOUNGER SELF

The advice I would give to myself when I was younger is don't be afraid to stick with what you have passion for. The second thing is just don't be afraid to stick with what's easy and what comes naturally to you.

I always got straight As in English and history, and I never had to study. But for science and math, I had to study, and I would get Bs in those subjects. Yet I chose food science as a major. I decided to do something that was hard. Maybe I should have done something that was a little bit easier and more within my own natural wheelhouse.

### ADVICE FOR THOSE SEEKING CAREER HAPPINESS

If I were to give advice to somebody who is not happy in their job, I would say, number one, if you have the time available, go take a vacation, and whatever it is you're fantasizing about—go do it or try to be close to whatever you're interested in.

I thought I wanted to be a yoga teacher, so I went and got certified to teach. Every teacher who taught me in my yoga training course was like, don't do it. They would tell me, "I like doing yoga; I don't like teaching it." Despite the warnings, I'm probably going to do it at some point just for kicks.

If you're trying to figure out what to do for a living, I say try it out if you have the time, if you have the energy—go see what it's like. Because a lot of times when we fantasize, we think we know what something is like. It's important not to make assumptions but to go explore it. Sometimes, you may decide to go work for a company for more money, but unfortunately, you don't always have the option to go to work for a company for two weeks to see what the culture is like.

The second thing is, depending on your resources, just remember you always have different choices. Try things— travel to other countries to see what other people are doing and talk to people you think are cool and interesting. And if you don't have time to go talk to people, try to study that stuff on your own time. Do that research and look at the things that seem interesting.

### TEN FEET DOWN THIRTY DIFFERENT ROADS

I've gone about ten feet down thirty different roads thinking these are things I want to do, then I say, "You know what? It doesn't feel right. Something about this doesn't match my gut."

I keep coming back and considering coaching. I keep coming back to that for some reason, and I'm not resisting it, but I'm not shutting the door. A lot of other doors have been shut for other reasons.

### GETTING RID OF THE "SHOULDS"

A decision isn't wrong if you're right with that decision at the time. No problem. Get rid of all those childhood messages about what you should or shouldn't do.

My mom apologized to me this weekend for telling me not to sing when I was young. She said I was a lot better than all these rock stars out here today. And I was like, that would have been really nice to hear when I was a kid. Because she shamed me when I was young, I never tried to sing even when I wanted to. Get rid of those "shoulds" and those artificial rules.

I'm happy with how things turned out. I'm happy I followed my passion about eighty percent of the time. And I'm proud of myself for doing that. It's just that now I want that extra little bit. I'm American, and I want it all, that's really what it is.

### EXERCISE: INVITING JOY INTO YOUR CAREER

Spend some time journaling on these questions:

- What do you love about your life? What are your passions?
- How much time are you able to commit to activities you're passionate about?
- How much does your career support what you're passionate about?
- Have you had to give up participating in activities you love due to your job? How does that make you feel?

- If you've had to give up some of your passions for your career, what would need to be done to enable you to do both?
- Is your passion woven into your career in some way? How satisfied are you with this?
- What "shoulds" are you living with in your life right now? What if you looked at the "shoulds" as choices instead? Does that feel different to you?
- How able are you to recognize that your happiness is important?
- How aligned are your values with those of your employer? If there's a gap, does that ever cause conflict? What, if anything, does that cost you?
- Are there organizations whose values align more closely with your own where you might enjoy working? What would you need to do to explore opportunities there?

# PART 4

# BECOMING A CHAMPION

**CHAPTER 11**

# COACHING:
# A Catalyst For
# Lasting Change

———

*It's not the strongest of the species that*
*survives, nor the most intelligent, but*
*the one most responsive to change.*

−LEON C. MEGGINSON[42]

It is frustrating when you are trying to reach a goal and fall short. You may be confused because you are working hard and using strategies that have worked for you in the past without getting the same results. When this happens, it's natural to look for an explanation.

———

42  Friedman, Thomas L. *Thank You for Being Late: An Optimist's Guide to Thriving in the Age of Accelerations* (Version 2.0, With a New Afterword). United States: Picador, 2017. p. 324.

Sometimes, a coworker may appear to be surpassing you due to an unfair advantage. Perhaps you feel like the cards must be stacked against you, because it seems like you've tried everything without achieving your goal. When this happens, you may even think something is wrong with *you*!

These responses are natural, based on the idea that you're seeing the whole picture and you understand how the workplace works. But as you know, work is a game, and if you're not winning, it's because you're playing by the wrong rules or your technique is off. A professional coach can help.

## WHAT IS COACHING?

The International Coach Federation defines coaching as "partnering with clients in a thought-provoking and creative process that inspires them to maximize their personal and professional potential."[43] The process focuses on the here and now rather than looking at the distant past or future. Its purpose is to help clients learn in their own way rather than teaching them a particular method.

## COMMON COACHING MISPERCEPTIONS

Coaching within business is a relatively new phenomenon, and misperceptions abound. I'll address some of the most common objections I've heard from people who desire the

---

43  International Coach Federation website. https://coachfederation.org/faqs?fwp_faqs_categories=global-coaching-and-mentoring-alliance-gc-ma&fwp_faqs_search=definition%20of%20coaching. Accessed January 25, 2020.

results that coaching can deliver but are skeptical about whether it will work for them.

**1. I GET GOOD ADVICE FOR FREE.**

Free advice is worth every penny you pay for it. I'm only half kidding. No doubt you have wise friends and family; however, it's difficult to separate the interests of your friends and loved ones from your own desires. Often, the advice you get from those close to you is colored by their own biases, desires, and fears for you and for themselves. In contrast, certified professional coaches are not attached to their clients' outcomes.

Working with an objective third party frees you to explore all options and to listen to your deepest thoughts and desires. This can be difficult to do with family and friends, especially if your goals conflict with theirs.

Coaching is action oriented. It's about moving toward your goals—not asking friends what they think you should do or venting over coffee to tolerate the status quo. The coach's role is to help you discover what you really want, then to work with you to develop a plan to achieve that goal.

**2. I HAVE A MENTOR, SO I DON'T NEED A COACH.**

Typically, mentors are experienced people who have already accomplished what you aspire to do. Usually you find them at work or within your network. You meet with them occasionally, fill them in on what you're up to, and get advice on situations you're dealing with.

Mentors are typically not paid and may be busy—meaning they don't always have time for you when you could use their counsel. They have "been there and done that" and typically use their own experience as the road map for how to direct you on your journey. But what happens when your journey takes a different turn or when your needs conflict with the availability (or opinion) of your mentor? A coach will help you find your own path, will not give advice, and will not be attached to the decisions you make for yourself.

Mentors often do not have the time or training to delve into identifying and removing your blocks in the same way that trained coaches do. Coaches and mentors both serve valuable roles, but they are not the same thing.

### 3. I CAN REACH MY GOALS ON MY OWN.

If you can identify your goals, develop plans to achieve them, identify and remove the blocks that stand in the way of success, hold yourself accountable for the deliverables along the way, and hit the deadlines you set for yourself, then you don't need a coach. My guess is that you wouldn't be reading this book if you had it all figured out, but only you know if that's true.

I've had clients who flirted with the idea of coaching but decided to try to reach their goals on their own because they didn't want to invest the money—only to come back later and hire me. It's not that you can't achieve your goals without a coach, but if you're trying to achieve something brand-new or high-stakes—or something that you've failed to do after many attempts—it may be wise to get professional help.

Blocks are often hard for you to see and overcome on your own. As I like to say, it's hard to read the label from inside the bottle.

### 4. COACHING IS A SCAM.

Many people in the marketplace call themselves coaches but have not received training and do not abide by the code of ethics set by the International Coach Federation (ICF).[44] When you work with a certified professional coach (CPC), you are working with someone who has been trained through an accredited ICF coach training program and has agreed to abide by the ICF code of ethics.

The training program that I completed through iPEC requires completion of more than three-hundred hours of training and passage of a certification exam that demonstrates an understanding of proven coaching techniques to support clients as they work toward their goals. Many coaches in the marketplace are not CPCs but *are* experienced and effective.

However, it can be difficult to tell the difference between those who are legitimate and effective and those who have simply adopted the title of "coach" without any training, experience, or certification. When shopping for a coach, find out what type of experience they have in assisting clients with challenges similar to what you're facing and ask for references.

---

44 International Coach Federation website. https://coachfederation.org/code-of-ethics. Accessed January 25, 2020.

## 5. A COACH NEEDS TO BE AN EXPERT ON MY SITUATION TO ADVISE ME.

True, no one will understand your situation as well as you do. Coaches are experts in coaching. You are the expert on you, and I believe you possess the ability to resolve any issue that arises in your life.

A coach's job is not to advise you. Our role is to support you as you explore, identify, and ultimately remove the blocks that hold you back from what you really want. Your coach can be there to help you brainstorm, give you space as you consider options and develop plans, and hold you accountable as you put your plans into action.

A coaching relationship is all about you. Think of your coach as your experienced wingman to make sure you keep moving in the direction of your goals.

## 6. COACHING WILL TAKE TOO LONG.

This objection reminds me of the Chinese proverb: "The best time to plant a tree was twenty years ago. The second-best time is now."

Coaching is about lasting change. If you want a quick change, you may be able to find an expert who can tell you exactly what you need to do now to make the changes you want, but ultimately, those changes will be what someone else thinks you need to do. You may find that, once the guru has left, you revert to old patterns because the underlying reasons for those patterns have not been addressed.

It's like when someone goes on a starvation diet to lose weight—they lose the pounds, but after the diet is over, all the weight comes back because the underlying poor eating habits were not addressed.

> *"The best time to plant a tree was twenty years ago. The second-best time is now."*
>
> —CHINESE PROVERB

### 7. I'VE BEEN SUCCESSFUL TO THIS POINT WITHOUT A COACH— WHY MESS WITH A GOOD THING?

Kudos to you for the success you've had. If you are happy with where you are and with the pace of your advancement, then you don't need a coach. But it's likely that what it will take to get to the next level is different from what it took to get where you are.

If you would like to move forward or are not sure which direction to go, a coach can be helpful. You may have blind spots in your awareness, and as you try to move ahead, you might keep running into invisible obstacles and be unable to see what's getting in the way. Experienced coaches have seen a lot of common behavior patterns and have techniques to uncover those blind spots and bring them into your awareness so the blocks can be avoided or broken through.

### 8. COACHING IS TOO EXPENSIVE.

Good coaching is a valuable investment. You can keep plugging along with what you've been doing and get the same results, or you can invest in yourself and get serious about working toward your goals. Perhaps you would like to be promoted but can't figure out why it hasn't happened yet.

A coach can work with you to identify what might be keeping you from getting to your goal—whether gaps in experience or skills or mindset blocks that stand in the way—and help you develop a plan to address the gaps or blocks.

To provide a simple dollar-and-cents example of the payback on coaching, if you invested three-thousand dollars to work with a coach and were able to get a promotion and a ten-thousand dollar raise, you'd net seven-thousand dollars in the first year. Over the course of five years, your three-thousand dollar investment could mean an additional fifty-thousand dollars in income with an ROI of more than fifteen times the initial investment—and that doesn't include other perks that might come with a promotion such as larger bonuses, raises based on a higher base salary, greater job satisfaction, and more.

I've had clients get a full return on their coaching investment in a matter of months, but I think the biggest returns have been in getting past blocks that had caused problems throughout their lives. Those types of transformations are truly priceless.

Sometimes, people are afraid to invest in coaching because they fear it won't work. The biggest factor in the impact of coaching is not the coach—it's the person's commitment to take action toward their goal. When people commit to taking action and are held accountable, they tend to get positive results.

## 9. TRULY TALENTED PEOPLE DON'T NEED COACHING.

It's interesting how often coaching clients wonder if they are the only ones who struggle with the things they do. When I get those questions, I always assure them that many successful people share the same worries they do. It can be tempting to look at a sleek and sophisticated business leader or charismatic professor who commands the attention of an auditorium full of people and believe they were born that way. Most of the time, that just isn't true.

The things that most people worry about are the same. The big differentiator is what they choose to do about it. What separates the very successful from everyone else is that they decided to take action to achieve their goals. They weren't just born that way.

Everyone is human. Even CEOs get coaching because it's impossible for everyone to be great at everything. As I've mentioned in other places in the book, what got you here is not going to get you to the next level. As you continue to learn and grow, you'll hit the limit on what's possible with your current knowledge, skills, and perspective. If you want to go beyond, you'll have to learn new things, and that's where coaches can help.

## 10. IT'S THE PEOPLE AROUND ME WHO NEED TO CHANGE.

For coaching to work, you must accept the truth that the only person you can change is yourself. Sometimes, a happy by-product of coaching is that people around you change in response to changes you've made because you've altered the dynamic of your interactions. When that happens, it can be amazing, but it's not something that you can count on.

Changing others is not a primary reason to pursue coaching. Coaching is about taking responsibility for your own life and stepping outside of your comfort zone to envision the life you want for yourself, then making the changes necessary for it to happen. Deciding to hire a coach and to commit to change is a personal decision and an individual journey.

## IF YOU DECIDE TO WORK WITH A COACH

Coaching is not for everyone. These five circumstances must be present for you to gain value from coaching:

1. You must believe change is possible.

2. You need to acknowledge that you are responsible for your own actions and situation.

3. You must commit to do the work needed to reach your goal.

4. You have to be willing to accept feedback.

5. You need to recognize that the coach is your partner during the journey but cannot do the work for you.

With an understanding of these ground rules, working with a coach can be a life-changing experience.

## LEARNING IN A SAFE ENVIRONMENT

My daughter is currently taking driving lessons. The car that she's learning in has a brake that the instructor can use to stop the car. Given that she's still a novice driver and is unsure in certain situations, it makes sense that the cars would be equipped with this feature.

Similarly, when individuals seek coaching, they are working toward a goal but would like a guide to help them navigate the path. They may feel confused about which direction to go because they've received a lot of input from external sources, which may cloud their ability to find their own path.

## SHIFTING THE CONTROLS TO YOU

A coach serves a role similar to that of my daughter's driving teacher. They are there to support the achievement of the client's goal. They understand the common fears and tendencies of people who want to learn a new way of operating. They help their clients develop the judgment to select and internalize the rules in a style that works best for them.

They are also there to allow the client to practice in a safe environment so that, eventually, they can continue on without that guidance—with more confidence and success than they would have achieved without the support. Ultimately, coaching is about helping people achieve their fullest potential.

As both a coach and a client of coaches, I can speak to the transformations that are possible with the support of a guide. With the help of a coach, I have been able to more easily achieve the goals I envisioned yet found I couldn't reach on my own. I've also seen people push past deep-rooted obstacles to enjoy success and satisfaction that had previously eluded them. Those kinds of breakthroughs are gratifying and not uncommon.

# JENNIFER: PAINTING
# A PERFECT CAREER

---

Jennifer C. Dowling is a university professor, an artist, a designer, and the author of the book *Multimedia Demystified*. Jennifer followed her heart and was true to her calling to be an artist while also allowing her curiosity about technology to guide her. She ended up getting in on the ground floor of a profession that didn't even exist when she started her quest.

You may think it doesn't make sense to follow your interests unless there's a clear path to monetizing them in your career. On Jennifer's journey, she met the people, developed the skills and knowledge, and was exposed to the opportunities that put her in the right place at the right time with the right skills to capitalize. Because of the newness of digital graphic technology at the time she was building her career, she would have had no way to plan it ahead of time.

## IN HER OWN WORDS

Someone recently called me a renaissance woman, which I feel is a much bigger honor than I deserve. I was just lucky enough to be on the ground floor of a lot of the tech stuff that is so common today. I wish I could say it was all part of a grand plan, but it wasn't. I just followed my interests and eventually ended up in a career that's perfect for me.

## BIG FAMILY, LITTLE HOUSE

As a kid, we had a big family and a small house, so there were always a lot of people around. I needed time on my own, so I would go off and play by myself. I liked to be outside in nature and I also liked drawing, making things, and reading. It was important for me to have time by myself when I could focus on creating.

My mother signed me up for a painting class when I was ten or eleven. A lady in the neighborhood taught the class in her basement, and she provided the paint and supplies. Nothing I did there looked like I'd become the next Picasso, but I enjoyed it.

## DOING WHAT I LIKED TO DO

When I got into high school, I took the studio art elective. It was a natural fit and by the end of school, I had a pretty good portfolio. When it was time to look at colleges, my mother encouraged me to consider those that offered studio art programs. She knew I liked it and was good at it. She wasn't worried about whether I'd get a job after graduation. I chose the University of New Hampshire, which has a strong studio art program.

I gravitated toward the things I liked to do. I never questioned that I had chosen the wrong college or major. I started getting pushback from fellow students in more practical areas of study like engineering and business who would ask, "What are you going to do with an art degree?" That was the first time I started to feel pressure about what I would do for a living.

## AN INTRODUCTION TO COMMERCIAL ART

I grew up in Rhode Island, and the summer between sophomore and junior year, I took two classes at Rhode Island School of Design that were life changing. One professor helped me get more in touch with my creativity, and the other professor helped me see that I'd need to be more committed to my art if I wanted to be really good.

## CREATING MY OWN PATH

When I went back to UNH in the fall, I told one of my fine art professors that I was interested in commercial art. He shunned it and said it wasn't "real" art. I realized, if I was interested in this path, that I was going to need to find out more on my own. To develop my commercial art skills, I joined the UNH student press.

I would be there at eleven o'clock at night, and the editors would give me assignments that I would have to draw right away. They would be standing outside the room and asking me, "Is it done yet?" The deadlines made me sweat, but I knew they would take my drawings and publish them in the newspaper. It was fun and helped me learn to work under pressure.

I got involved in the Student Committee on Popular Entertainment that organized concerts and brought in big groups like Santana, Patti Smyth, the B-52's, and J. Geils Band. I made all the posters and flyers for the concerts, which gave me some experience in marketing. I had to balance making them look good but also doing them quickly. It forced me to confront my tendency toward perfectionism.

### GETTING FIRED FROM MY FIRST JOB

After graduation, I went home to live with my mom and got a job with a printing company. The owner assumed I had more experience than I did, and she didn't have time to train me, so she let me go. Being fired from my first full-time job was crushing, because I failed. The owner implied that I had misrepresented my capabilities, and I guess I did, but I didn't know what I didn't know. It made me question whether I wanted to do commercial art after all.

### MOM'S DIAGNOSIS AND A ROLE REVERSAL

I was between jobs when my mother found out that she had breast cancer. With her diagnosis, I experienced a big shift in my priorities. I had planned to move to Boston, but I couldn't because my mother needed me. My father had died years before, and I had to care for her and take her to her radiation appointments.

She was scared and all of a sudden, we had a role reversal. I felt like I was the "parent" and started to experience severe anxiety and mild depression because my sole focus was on helping my mom through this illness and I didn't know where my own future was headed.

## CLARIFYING WHAT I WANTED

This was the start of what became a repeating pattern in my career. When I had setbacks, I'd ask myself, "What do I want?", "What do I need to find out about?", and "What do I want to pursue?"

I had graduated in May, my mom was diagnosed in June, and I helped her through treatments for the rest of the year. Thankfully, the treatments worked, and she went into remission. By February of the next year, I moved to Boston and accepted a job in the circulation department at a publishing company.

I had an idea that I'd be able to move into the graphic design department after I established myself there. I got really good at data entry, but I felt like a little peon.

After eighteen months, I was comfortable, but I had no opportunities to move into a more creative role. I made some nice friends, but I didn't want to stay in circulation for the rest of my career. I needed to move on.

## DISCOVERING COMPUTER GRAPHICS

Around that time, in 1987 or 1988, I saw an article in *Providence Journal* about a design studio that was doing computer graphics and animation. It's hard to imagine now, but computer graphics software was cutting-edge technology at the time. I was intrigued, so I called the company to learn more. That call got me some freelance graphic design work from them, which eventually led to a full-time job.

The agency's primary client was a trailblazer in tech—Lotus Development Corporation. I was designing templates for the Lotus Freelance Graphics software program. The agency eventually closed the small office I was in and laid me off. I was in tears when I found out, but I began to see these disruptions as events that led to new and better opportunities.

### EXPLORING OPTIONS POOLSIDE

It was summer, so I collected unemployment and hung out by the pool trying to figure out my next move. I liked computer graphics, but I didn't know if that was the right path for me. I did some freelance graphics work for a hospital.

I explored becoming an art teacher, because one of my mother's best friends was an art teacher and a childhood mentor of mine. I volunteered at an after-school program, then took a summer position as a camp director teaching art. I liked it well enough, but I wasn't getting paid much. I had a positive experience and I thought I could do it, but a lot of teachers were getting pink slips at the time. I would probably have to go someplace far away to get a job teaching art, and I didn't want to take that chance.

### THE MOST BANG FOR MY BUCK

Whatever I decided to do, I wanted to get the most bang for my buck. I didn't want to focus too much on just one thing that may or may not make me happy. I decided to go back to school for a Master of Fine Arts degree, because I'd have the credentials to teach college, work in a design agency, or both.

I enrolled full time at what is now University of Massachusetts, Dartmouth. As a first-year graduate student, I got an assistantship teaching a design class for undergrads. I learned through that experience that teaching at the college level was hard, and I didn't want to teach unless I knew more. I was considering a path toward teaching fine arts, but I also liked working on the computer.

## TEACHING, TECHNOLOGY, AND ART INTERSECT

In the late 1980s, before attending grad school, I went to computer animation film festivals around Boston that showed Pixar short films before anyone had ever heard of Pixar. That's where my interest in 3D computer graphics started.

Later, I saw an interactive exhibit at the Boston Museum of Science that I thought was the coolest thing in the world. You could click on animated graphic scenes within this desert habitat. It was interactive art using computers to teach. It hit on all the things I was interested in—teaching, computers, art. I began to think this was the right path for me.

My grad school advisor taught interactive multimedia and computer animation very early after their inception. He helped me get my first job doing graphical user interface design through a graduate assistantship working on a math educational computer program for children.

## EDUCATIONAL INTERACTIVE MULTIMEDIA

Over time, I decided to focus my graduate studies on designing educational, interactive multimedia. I developed an interactive program for children that focused on science—it was an educational game for kids.

It's funny to think back on it, because programs like that are so ubiquitous now, but at the time, they were just starting to bubble up in the consumer market. I was graduating with this knowledge and these skills at a great time.

### LOTS OF OPPORTUNITY

After graduation in 1994, I worked a variety of freelance jobs in Boston. I had picked a great path for myself. I had so much opportunity to apply the things I'd learned with my freelance clients at the time. My projects ranged from developing graphic icons for foreign language software to working on graphic videos at MIT. It was awesome. I loved what I was doing, and I assumed it was leading to a creative job in the business world.

### RIGHT PLACE, RIGHT TIME, RIGHT BACKGROUND

My husband and I married in 1995 and moved out of Boston into the suburbs. I still worked for several freelance clients in the city, but of course, the commute was much less convenient then.

I learned of a position teaching computer graphics at a state university near our new home. Because the subject was so new, frankly, I don't think many people had the background to teach the topic.

I had my master's degree with a focus on computer graphics and interactive design. We lived close to the university and the role seemed like a good fit for me. I had taught schoolkids, at the college level as a teaching assistant in grad school, and had also led computer design workshops.

I applied and I got the job. I was in the right place with the right experience at the right time. I just walked right into a tenure-track position. I didn't realize at the time how fortunate I was.

## A PERFECT FIT

It's been almost twenty-five years since I started teaching at the college level, and it's been great for me. As a professor, I have a good balance of structure and freedom. I have a lot of control over my time and what I teach. There's a lot of variety and I get to work with a lot of different kinds of students. I get the summers off, so I can spend time with my family and work on my own creative projects.

My advice to anyone looking for more in their career is to pay attention to where they get fulfillment. It's important to feel positive about and challenged by what you do for a living.

## FOLLOWING WHAT MADE ME HAPPY

When I was moving up in my career and exploring, if I saw something I thought was interesting, I would reach out to the company to learn more. I was offered internships and jobs simply for contacting companies that did things I was interested in. My curiosity served me well.

Throughout my career, I moved forward even though I was nervous at times. I'm not a quitter, but I figured if I didn't like something, I could always leave. I faced my challenges and I kept pushing.

Getting to where I am has been the result of a variety of decisions. Some were probably not great, but they helped form who I am today. A little bit of disappointment can make you push more for the kinds of things that might make you happy. I didn't specifically know what I wanted when I was twenty-three, but I kept looking, and I certainly understand what makes me happy now.

### EXERCISE: WHAT MAKES YOU HAPPY?

Give some thought to these questions and answer them in your journal. Read back over your answers and see what insights you get about yourself and what you need to be happy in your life and career:

- When you were a child, what did you like to do?
- What did you want to do when you grew up? Are you doing it now? If not, why not?
- How willing are you to ask for the accommodations you need to make yourself happy?
- Have you ever overstayed in a job you didn't like due to fear of the unknown?
- Have you ever been steered away from a career you enjoyed—by yourself or someone else—because it wasn't considered practical? If so, what examples exist of people making a living in that career?

- If you're interested in a career, who could you talk to in your network who can tell you more about it? Who can introduce you to someone doing that job?
- What, if anything, keeps you from pursuing a job or career that you would enjoy more than what you're doing currently? How true are the reasons you tell yourself for why you don't take action?
- What action would you need to take to move closer to a career you would enjoy?
- When you're ninety years old, how do you think you'll look back on your present career? With pride or regret or another emotion?

# CHAPTER 12

# WINNING THE GAME OF WORK: Playing By Your Own Rules

———

*Our doubts are traitors, and make us lose the good we oft might win, by fearing to attempt.*

–WILLIAM SHAKESPEARE, *MEASURE FOR MEASURE*[45]

I hope you're beginning to understand work differently and feel more empowered in your choices as they relate to your career. When you started this book, maybe you were experiencing a mismatch between what you wanted out of your career and what you thought you had to put in to get it.

———

45 Mowat, Dr. Barbara A., Shakespeare, William. *Measure for Measure.* United Kingdom: Simon & Schuster, 2005. p. 35.

I hope your perspective has shifted at least a little so you realize that you don't have to settle for someone else's estimation of your worth and someone else's judgment of your potential. I hope you've embraced the fact that what you want out of your life and career matters.

## THINGS ARE JUST AS THEY ARE

The bottom line is that things are just as they are. We choose the lens through which we view things to determine whether they are good or bad. We can choose to be grateful for the things that go well and learn from the things that don't without any shame or chastisement. When we beat ourselves up over so-called mistakes, we're wasting energy that could be used for actual productive activities.

I want to be clear with you that beating yourself up is not a productive activity. You can just as easily remember lessons learned from a mistake without the additional burden of shame. In fact, shame can make you avoid similar activities in the future for fear of making another mistake—because of the discomfort of your self-judgment for making the mistake rather than the mistake itself.

You can always forgive yourself and go forward unburdened. It's your choice.

## THE FIVE RULES FOR WINNING THE GAME

Throughout the book, I've shared stories from inspiring professionals who sought more satisfaction and authenticity from work. In some cases, their efforts resulted in making more money or gaining a more elevated position, yet that wasn't their true goal. In each case, the people I interviewed were seeking a career that was aligned more closely with who they were as people.

This book contains lots of tips, tricks, and stories about how to get ahead in your career, but in a nutshell, moving toward a career you love is how you win the game of work.

### 1. KNOW YOURSELF.

Determine what you like to do and what you're good at. Listen closely to what your intuition tells you is your true purpose, then go out and find opportunities to live that purpose. You may need to go out and try a few—or a lot—of things to pinpoint your purpose.

Your purpose may change over time, and that's okay. Just stay in touch with yourself so you know when you're aligned with your purpose and when you're not. Then make changes accordingly.

### 2. KNOW HOW YOU ADD VALUE.

For-profit organizations value three primary areas: revenue generation, cost savings, and risk reduction. When you take an inventory of what you do, make sure you can articulate them using the PAR method: what was the *problem*, what *action* did you take, and what was the *result*? As much as possible, *quantify* your results and tie them to one of the areas that organizations value.

### 3. CLARIFY YOUR OPTIONS.

Listen closely to your own inner voice. What do you enjoy doing? Brainstorm on what activities would provide you with the satisfaction you'd like to receive from your career. Try not to edit yourself as you go through this process. After you've listened closely to what you'd like to do, then spend some time looking at the gaps between where you are and where you'd like to be.

If you don't know what you don't know, find someone who is doing a role of interest to you and interview them. Find out if the reality aligns with your vision of your future career. Find out what skills, training, experience, and temperament are required to be successful in that role. Once you have a clear view of the gaps, you can build a plan to bridge the gaps and move toward achieving that goal.

### 4. NURTURE RELATIONSHIPS EVERY DAY.

While most people focus primarily on skills and experience when managing their career, relationships are arguably even more important. People hire people, and they tend to hire people they know, like, and trust. Carve out time to invest in building relationships, especially with those closest to you.

We can often take for granted the people we work with every day, yet they are our strongest and most powerful connections because they know us well. Take the time to build your LinkedIn profile to all-star status and get connected with everyone you work with.

At some point in the future, you will likely go your separate ways, yet you can continue to support each other's career development on many fronts—hiring, buying or selling from each other, exchanging industry information, and so forth.

As you meet new people, make it habit to invite them to get LinkedIn with you so you are continually expanding your network. The investment will serve you well as you progress in your career. Likewise, carve out time to nurture these relationships through calls, notes, coffees, and lunches.

### 5. TAKE IMPERFECT ACTION.

For many high achievers, the tendency can be to analyze and look for the "perfect" path forward. Because the future is unwritten, there is *no* perfect path. Factors around us are constantly evolving, and even a course of action that worked in the past may not work the same way going forward. Take an action, learn from it, and use what you learn to optimize your next step. To meet your goals, take productive action. Continue to test, learn, and optimize. As Nelson Mandela[46] once said,

*"I never lose. I always win or learn."*

Even if you fall on your face, you're still moving forward!

### OVERCOMING SELF-DOUBT

The trick to overcoming self-doubt and owning your confidence is to recognize a few key truths:

46  Schleckser, Jim. "Nelson Mandela's Secret to Winning." https://www.inc.com/jim-schleckser/nelson-mandela-s-secret-to-winning.html. June 21, 2016. Accessed February 1, 2020.

## 1. YOU ARE PERFECT THE WAY YOU ARE.

Your innate worth is not tied in any way to your performance rating (or your GPA). You are a worthy human being regardless of someone else's judgment. You possess unique intelligence and capabilities. Even if you make a mistake, you'll figure out how to fix it.

Free yourself of the fear of external judgment. You'll be amazed at how light and nimble you are without constant self-consciousness. Worrying eats up the energy you'll need to respond if something occasionally goes wrong.

> *"If a problem is fixable, if a situation is such that you can do something about it, then there is no need to worry.*
>
> *If it's not fixable, then there is no help in worrying. There is no benefit in worrying whatsoever."*
>
> —THE 14TH DALAI LAMA[47]

## 2. YOUR OWN VALIDATION IS ALL THAT MATTERS.

I'm not suggesting that you not face things you could do better—that would be a form of denial. You need to take responsibility. However, don't berate yourself or feel guilty because you aren't perfect.

---

47  Piburn, Sidney D. *Dalai Lama: A Policy of Kindness.* India: Motilal Banarsidass Publishers Pvt. Limited, 2002. p. 40.

Preserve any energy you may use to tell yourself you're "not good enough" and use it to fix the problem. Forgive yourself for not being omnipotent.

### 3. THE "RULES" OF THE WORKPLACE AND SCHOOL ARE DIFFERENT.

The challenges you face at work are often new and undefined. It's up to you to define parameters, identify risks, and decide how you'll plan and execute. Your boss is counting on you to know your stuff. He or she often doesn't know the day-to-day challenges you face and expects you to make decisions based on the best knowledge you have at the moment.

Unlike in school, no wise teacher will grade you on each stage of your project. I know you know this, but there may be a part inside that is still trying to be the teacher's pet and do everything perfectly. This is impossible and a hindrance in the workplace, as there is no "perfect" path. You just gotta get stuff done!

### 4. YOU DEFINE YOUR OWN SUCCESS (AND FAILURE).

Granted, the rewards you reap may not be the ones you desire if your goal doesn't align with those in charge, but sometimes, your own self-respect and validation is worth much more. Likewise, if you decide to look at mistakes as learning opportunities, even failure can be a success.

## THE FUTILITY OF PERFECTION

As Ukrainian-Canadian poet Vironika Tugaleva[48] states,

*"There is no way to genuinely, powerfully,
truly love yourself while crafting
a mask of perfection."*

You are what you are, and by trying to hide behind a mask of perfection, you hide yourself from those who might love and appreciate you. If the mask is pleasing to others, it's still not satisfying, because what they admire is not the real you.

## EVOLVING EXPECTATIONS

I'd been a corporate marketer for large banks for decades, and in that context, I had access to a large budget and used advertising agencies and video producers to create our branded content. When I started my coaching business and began making videos, out of habit, I still had my big bank marketer hat on but without the large marketing department to support my vision.

At first, I didn't realize that perhaps I should adapt my expectations for my videos. I attempted to replicate the quality of what I'd been used to at the bank by buying software and teaching myself advanced video editing techniques. It didn't take me long to recognize that, as a solopreneur, it would be

---

48 Tugaleva, Vironika. The Art of Talking to Yourself: Self-Awareness Meets the Inner Conversation. Canada: Soulux Press, 2017.

impossible to replicate corporate quality with my budgetary and time constraints.

Out of necessity, I started shooting videos on my iPhone and posting them within minutes so I could get on to other more important work. To my surprise, what I found was that people actually preferred the quick and dirty videos. People could relate to me. They liked my message and were tuning in and watching the videos that were shot wherever I happened to be.

I took off the mask, and guess what? People actually liked what they saw. What a relief and confidence builder. I still sometimes have a moment of trepidation before I post a video—what if I look like a complete dork? What if people believe a coach should be put together at all times? What if . . . what if . . . what if . . .

I finally came to the conclusion that, if someone thinks those things, they probably aren't going to be a good a client for me. I did the corporate thing for a long time, and I don't dress for the boardroom when I work from home, so if that's what someone's expectation is, we probably won't be a good fit. It feels good to release the self-judgment and need for perfection and just be me!

## LET YOUR MISTAKES BE YOUR GUIDE
A realization that has dawned on me as I've gotten older is one that's pretty darn profound:

*You cannot make a mistake!*

Take a moment to let that sink in.

What would you do if you believed that were really true? How would you feel? Take a deep breath and close your eyes and really feel it. Maybe you have a sense of freedom and relief. Maybe you feel unburdened and notice a little bubble of happiness rising within you. You might even feel a little scared about how powerful that would make you. You could literally do anything you wanted.

> *"Our deepest fear is not that we are inadequate.*
> *Our deepest fear is that we are powerful*
> *beyond measure.*
> *It is our light, not our darkness,*
> *that most frightens us."*

—MARIANNE WILLIAMSON[49]

## GETTING OUTSIDE THE BOX

It's natural that if we've lived our whole lives inside a box, freedom in the vast universe might feel scary. Maybe the thought of it releases a mental cavalry that thunders into your consciousness, bringing a tiny but persistent Napoleonic voice that bellows, "*Whoa!* Not so fast! Of course you're tremendously flawed, and it's ridiculous to think you

---

49  Williamson, Marianne. *A Return to Love.* United Kingdom: Thorsons, 1996. p. 165.

cannot make a mistake. You made a dozen mistakes before lunch today!"

*"It's ridiculous to think you cannot make a mistake. You made a dozen before lunch today!"*

As Williamson alludes to in her poem—the light is blinding! But you can deal with it. Put on your imaginary shades and thank the little voice for stating its opinion. Yes, *opinion.* That's what the little voice is sharing with you. The little voice is your gremlin we met in Chapter 7 and is not the authority on your truth.

The gremlin's role has been to protect you since you were a baby and were learning about how to get along in this chaotic and imperfect world. Every time you experienced an unpleasant effect, the gremlin jotted down a "rule" to keep you safe.

I see a couple problems with that situation. First, when the gremlin started making the rules, it had the intellect of a baby. Being a baby, it would sometimes misconstrue situations and assum you had caused the outcome when, in fact, it was caused by something else entirely. This resulted in you following a rule, perhaps for decades, based on false assumptions.

## UPPING YOUR GAME

We're used to seeing coaches lead and develop players on professional sports teams. They know the game and understand what actions lead to winning outcomes. They watch the players and provide feedback to them so they are more aware of habits that prevent them from winning—whether a batter swinging too soon or a gymnast beginning her dismount too far from the end of the balance beam—it can be difficult for the person engaged in the activity to see it clearly enough to change without a coach's input and support.

Coaches do not play the game for their players. I've yet to see an NFL coach throw off his headset and run into the game to replace the quarterback after he threw an interception. The players have to play their own game, even when things are not going according to plan. The coaches call different plays, encourage effort, and will review the films with the team after a game. Then they'll decide what to do differently next time.

I've seen huge mindset shifts that have led to meaningful wins with clients. Heavy weights have been set down forever. Big hurdles have been surmounted to reach stretch goals. Limiting beliefs have been replaced by brand-new attitudes of enduring optimism and confidence. Coaching can be life-changing.

### UPDATE YOUR "RULES" AS NEEDED

Rules that were appropriate for you as a child may no longer be appropriate for you as an adult, but most of us are not aware of these "rules," and we rarely check the rulebook to see if they need to be updated. Therefore, the gremlin keeps sending messages that you are making mistakes and you're not doing it "right"—whatever "it" is.

Unfortunately, because we're not consciously aware, this gremlin can act like a merciless dictator. You feel guilty or wrong or imperfect, and you may not even realize why. As stated in the previous chapter, it can help to name your gremlin so you can recognize where these messages are coming from.

The gremlin acts out of fear, truly believes those faulty rules will keep you safe, and will try to make you feel guilty to control you. However, if you update those rules, you no longer need to feel bad.

The gremlin is persistent, and the next volley may be something like, "The world has made rules that you need to follow to live a successful life. You're on that path and you must stay on that path. Period." What a little tyrant the gremlin is! Again, thank the gremlin for its opinion. The future is unwritten, and if you're here on earth right now, playing the game of work (and of life), you're invited to decide on and play by your own rules.

## STEPPING FULLY INTO YOUR POWER

You—wonderful, unique you—are on this earth for a reason, and that reason is to be *you*! When you are unapologetically yourself, you will find others are drawn to you more. It's refreshing when people are authentic, quirky, imperfect, joyful, and interesting. When you are afraid but go forward anyway, you pave the path for others to show their true selves.

Absolutely no one is in a position to judge whether your contribution is good enough or right. Even people who think they know what's right for you can't see the big picture and understand what your purpose is here on earth. It's up to you to determine that.

While it may be a breath of fresh air to recognize that you are freer than you'd previously known, it can be overwhelming to realize you can always choose from nearly endless courses of action.

I am not saying all of them are great or that there won't be consequences, but you have options. Some of the actions you hadn't considered, or told yourself you couldn't do for one reason or another, may yield the results you desire. Recognize you always have a choice. You may not like the consequences that come along with the choices in front of you, but you are free to choose.

## ONLY ONE WAY TO WIN

The games we play are just an illusion. Each of us determines our own rules. What I hope you take away from the book is that you matter and what you want matters. Your presence right here and right now matters, and you have an obligation to step as fully as possible into your full potential according to your own definition. Step back so you get a broader perspective of what's possible and recognize your choices are infinite.

In every moment, you can choose a new direction. Even when you may feel trapped, you are surrounded by possibility. Embrace it, and you'll be well on your way to winning not only the game of work, but also the game of life.

# HOW THE GAME IS CHANGING: An Interview With Gary A. Bolles

———

Gary A. Bolles is an internationally-recognized expert on the future of work and learning. His focus is on the strategies for helping individuals, organizations, communities, and countries to thrive in the transition to a digital work economy. He is cofounder of eParachute.com, which helps job hunters and career changers from youth to over age fifty with online and in-person programs.

He trained as a career counselor at age nineteen, and he's an expert on effective methods for job hunters and career changers from *What Color is Your Parachute?* This best-selling career book of all time was authored by his father, Richard N. Bolles.

As chair for the Future of Work for Singularity University, Gary A. Bolles leads the organization's efforts to empower a global community with the mindset, skillset, and network to create an abundant future of work and learning. In the seismic transition to what Bolles calls the digital work economy, individuals, organizations, communities, and countries all need to develop a shared understanding of the dynamics of disruptive change, collaborate on the development of effective strategies, and ensure all people have access to meaningful work and lifelong learning opportunities. Bolles has also authored a series of video courses on the future of work for LinkedIn Learning.

As a partner in the boutique consulting agency Charrette LLC, Bolles helps clients identify and understand trends affecting their organizations and markets through strategic conferences, innovation consulting, strategy design charrettes, and collaborative initiatives.

Bolles has served as a strategic consultant and visiting lecturer for clients such as Google, Intel, the New Zealand government, and the United Nations. He has also cofounded a variety of conferences and strategic initiatives and has served as a consulting producer for strategic events for Google, Singularity University, TED, and London Business School. Formerly, Bolles was the editorial director of technology publications for Yahoo! Internet Life, Inter@ctive Week, and Network Computing, as well as the on-screen host of TechTV's *Working the Web*.

## THE MEANING OF WORK

**INTERVIEWER:** I believe that, ideally, everyone would like to be happy and find meaning at work. Your father's book *What Color is Your Parachute?* was first published in 1970. With this and so many other tools available to job seekers and career changers, why do you think it's not more common for people who aren't happy with their careers to proactively seek work they would enjoy more?

**BOLLES:** This whole area of happiness at work is fraught, because the word is very much a code. I often talk about the "old rules" of work—your parents or grandparents often had a more traditional approach. Their attitude was, "Why should your work make you happy? Work is about feeding your family and putting a roof over their heads. That's happiness. That's fulfillment." That's the older model.

My father talked a lot about this at various points in *What Color is Your Parachute?* He edited and rewrote it every year. He talked about the Puritan mentality and how some people don't look to work to bring them purpose or happiness. That's why we call it work—look in the dictionary. It's helpful to explore the language—it matters a lot. Oftentimes, in the context of work, I don't even talk about purpose or even happiness. Instead, I'll use the word "meaning," which seems to be the word people react to the least negatively. Because you can find meaning in anything—you can find meaning in a flower, in a poem.

## What do you feel you're on the planet Earth to do?

In all my years doing workshops, I've found that it is very helpful for people to explore the language and their thoughts around work. Specifically, examining the various aspects of themselves, asking, "What do you feel you're on the planet Earth to do?" Some people want work and their purpose to be separate. They want to make money at work, and then their meaning and happiness may come from volunteer activities or from their families. So it's a journey toward the target.

Some people define themselves as unhappy based on the things they have or don't have. Another insight is that, because people have such different approaches, it makes sense to offer them a range of options. Some people like the self-assessments and tests because they want a definitive answer.

The first reason that people often don't think about self-inventory as a way of understanding their own skills, experiences, and knowledge and putting them into some sort of context is that nobody trained them to do that. Secondly, nobody provided you with a user manual on *you*. When you were born, nobody told you what you were optimized for.

> ### When you were born, nobody told you what you were optimized for.

We're all trial-and-error machines, and we have to figure this stuff out for ourselves. It can be hard work. That's why some people avoid therapy; they don't want to do the hard work.

Some people prefer tests, because they just want somebody to give them the answer.

What we find is that we need to go to where the people are and help them expand their thinking. So it's a matter of mindset and skillset. The mindset of "yes, you can do this" and the skillset of providing the techniques so they can do this work.

My own bias, and my father shared it, is we haven't typically guided people toward assessments. They can be wonderful and if they help someone find answers and that works for them, more power to them. We just find that it helps to have a range of different options and let people choose.

Depending upon the population, what you're gonna find is that some people will be automatically drawn to this approach. Some people like the more structured and mechanistic approaches—they want a methodology or a framework that gives them a language.

It's one of the reasons people like Myers-Briggs, for instance, because there's language that you can use to describe yourself—"You're an ENTJ and I'm an INTP"—and it helps them understand it.

## SATISFACTION AND THE "STRIVING CULTURE"

INTERVIEWER: I've observed that many high achievers embrace the "rules" they learned in school because that's what helped them be successful, yet when they get into the workforce, they may continue looking for the "perfect" answer to the challenges they face and may lose sight of what's going on around them.

They may be so intensely goal-oriented that they lose touch with their inner compass. Even when these "rules" no longer serve them well and what they thought would lead to a "successful career" isn't working, they may have a hard time doing things differently.

What are your thoughts on this striving culture?

**BOLLES:** Typically, people will build a model of what they think success looks like based on whatever influences they've had in their lives—parents, school, society. They use this framework when they are young to drive toward this vision of "success." People assume that there's an implicit agreement with the universe, and if they achieve it, then they'll be happy.

When they get there and they're not happy, they'll ask, "What is this? Who screwed up? Did I screw up? Did society screw up?" They believe that these accomplishments are going to bring them happiness—money, power, position, success—then they get there and they don't feel that. Plenty of people achieve those things and they do feel happy, but that's not always the case. Some understandable insights come out of this.

*People assume that there's an implicit agreement with the universe, and if they achieve it, then they'll be happy.*

Often, when people are very driven, they don't take time for introspection. And a whole bunch of things change in them emotionally and psychologically over the years, and they may not take time to step back and understand these changes.

It's part of the success model. If one doesn't do the stepping-back process and ask if this is really what they want out of their life and consciously recognize the elements they are looking for, it can cause problems. When people do consider "success," it's normally not holistic. It's very career-centric. It's based on messages that society gives us about what success should be like. I think the opportunity here is to give people a safe place to take a breath and do a self-inventory.

*You're looking back at the past filtered through your perception of the present to plan for the future.*

−RICHARD N. BOLLES

My father was fond of saying that you're looking back at the past filtered through your perception of the present to plan for the future. It's helpful for people to step back and ask what they have done and how they feel about it.

My dad wrote a book, *The Three Boxes of Life*, that is focused on a more holistic model—it's not just about what you do for work, but it's also what you learned in school and what you do in your leisure time. It's the integration of all those things, and it's a very valuable exercise for people to go through.

You've got to look back and find peace with what you've done so far. The type As will say they're never satisfied, so they'll say they didn't do enough. You've got to invest in anchors. That's the way I think about it—your values are your anchors. You've got to revisit and instantiate your values.

What are the things that you believe will make you happy? How can you test that thesis? And then, how can you commit yourself to a roadmap where you'll continue to have more of that feeling and be intentional about it?

You've got to look at all aspects of your life—education, leisure, work—whatever you want to include as part of your model. Work will always thanklessly take over your entire life if you let it.

The other things that tend to take over your life are bad things that you may not have much control over like health issues, loss of a spouse, or divorce. These are the things where life raps you on the head and says, "Now you're screwed."

## CLINGING TO THE OLD RULES AT YOUR PERIL

**INTERVIEWER:** With all of the changes that have taken place in the economy over the past, say, twenty years, what are the implications for the next generation of workers?

**BOLLES:** One more area that I'd like to address. A lot of type-A parents are about to ruin the next generation . . . they're following the rules of work that they used to reach their own level of success, and then they apply it to their kids. What they don't recognize is that it is a completely different world. Parents will ask me all the time, especially when kids are at that inflection point of seventeen and thinking about college, "How can we help our kid to be happy and successful?"

The first thing you need to do is drop "successful," because that comes from the parents' model. It's their definition. When they say they want their kids to go to the "right" school and study the "right" field and get the "right" job—all those "rights" are from the parents' model, and it is ruining their children.

*A lot of type-A parents are about to ruin the next generation . . . they're following the rules of work that they used to reach their own level of success, and then they apply it to their kids.*

The basic premise is, if you want your kids to be happy, then everything that we've been talking about is what we need to be teaching them. We should teach them how to do a self-inventory so they understand their own unique skills and values. We've got to help them to put the pieces together, because this next generation will more likely operate in a very nontraditional work context. They might not have a day job. For example, they may be driving for Uber and working on a startup with friends. I call it a portfolio of work.

The contract between this next generation and traditional employers is going to continue to erode. They are going to think of themselves more as free agents. All of the things that parents are doing to shoehorn them into the old model of success and happiness that worked for the older generation is going to screw up the next generation because things have changed and will continue to change.

## TECH GIVETH AND TECH TAKETH AWAY

**INTERVIEWER:** How has technology impacted the state of work and people's ability to operate successfully in the gig economy? How do you see it supporting people's ability to make a living that can also support increased happiness and fulfillment through work?

**BOLLES:** I've been deeply focused on the future of work issues for about half-a-dozen years, and I have developed opinions after talking to a lot of really interesting people. According to my father's three boxes model, people divided their lives into a big chunk of education, a big chunk of work, and a big chunk of leisure, the period formerly known as retirement. That model worked reasonably well in the period from post–World War II until the late 1990s. In the current world of exponential change driven by technology, work is being continually unbundled, and now we have a whole set of techniques for managing this kind of portfolio environment that we never had before.

Our kids are going through an educational system that is calibrated toward one person, one job, but then they graduate into a world of work that is no longer like that. Essentially, we're failing our kids. We're not giving them techniques to succeed in this new work environment. Because the internet evaporates roles in the middle, there are fewer and fewer middle-skill jobs. There's more at the top and there's a lot of stuff at the bottom that is at a very high risk of being globalized.

*Our kids are going through an educational system that is calibrated toward one person, one job, but then they graduate into a world of work that is no longer like that.*

The good news is that what technology taketh away, technology giveth back. Technology reduces the friction to entry in any arena. For example, your kids can work on video production projects that they wouldn't have been able to do previously without ten years of experience and equipment they could never afford. Today, technology empowers them to do an HD movie on their cell phone.

Because the barriers to entry have been reduced in so many arenas, it's an egalitarian golden age. There is more opportunity on the bottom end to enter so many different fields, but we've not taught our kids how to manage that. There are a ton of distractions. A lot of workers, not just kids, are juggling work portfolios, and we haven't given them the techniques to manage that well.

In this type of work environment, from an earnings standpoint, what you end up getting is a fever chart. It's not a straight line of earning where you get a predictable amount in a paycheck every two weeks. In today's work portfolio environment, you draw a baseline of your average income over time, and when the actual earnings (the fever line) are below that, you're in the red, and when it's above, you're in the black.

Today, people who work in this fashion, which is increasingly common, are continually jumping above that line, and in some cases, making a lot of money. Then literally the next month, they have no money. We haven't helped people manage that at all. It's really just basic finance stuff.

We've got to teach them how to save and how to get the best pay for their work so they don't take anything that is offered to them. We've got to give them all these techniques, or what will end up happening is that people may be doing the things they love to do, but their efforts don't lead to a sustainable income.

### JUST-IN-TIME LEARNING

**INTERVIEWER:** So it sounds like you're saying part of the equation that may be missing is an understanding of finance and marketing, so people can not only follow their passions, but also make a profit. Technology has been a boon in many ways, and I've observed that it has also taken the place of mentors in many cases.

Today, technology is so inexpensive and accessible that young people can find resources, then go to YouTube to learn to do things without the help of an older person to teach them. In the past, this wouldn't have been possible.

What are your thoughts on this?

**BOLLES:** Today, learning is "just in time" and "just in con-text." You don't have to go back and get a four-year degree to be able to do certain types of work. In many cases, you can just start doing whatever it is immediately, and all you need is the information to solve this specific problem and nothing more. That's an advantage in many ways, but what can be lost is the connectivity and context.

We're living in a very interesting time. The models of the past need to evolve to be aligned with the realities of today's workplace.

\* \* \*

*If you would like to learn more about how to be ready for the workplace of tomorrow, Gary A. Bolles has developed a series of courses that are available on LinkedIn Learning that address topics such as change, learning agility, the new rules of work, and more.*

# APPENDIX

———

**INTRODUCTION**

3  Wilson, Sarah K. L. Dragon School: Sworn. N.p.: INDEPENDENTLY PUBLISHED, 2018.

**CHAPTER 1**

4  "Yogi Berra Quote." Quotefancy.com. Accessed February 1, 2020. https://quotefancy.com/quote/941643/Yogi-Berra-Nothing-is-like-it-seems-but-everything-is-exactly-like-it-is

5  Posnanski, Joe. "The Meaning of Yogi: It's déjà vu all over again." Sports Illustrated, July 4, 2011, pp. 64-66.

6  Berra, Yogi. *The Yogi Book*. Workman Publishing, 1998, p. 9.

**CHAPTER 2**

7  Lao Tzu Quotes. Goodreads.com. Accessed January 25, 2020. https://www.goodreads.com/quotes/4304-at-the-center-of-your-being-you-have-the-answer.

[8] DeLong, Thomas J. *Flying Without a Net: Turn Fear of Change into Fuel for Success.* Harvard Business Review Press, 2011. p. x (preface).

[9] Sarah Green, "The Hidden Demons of High Achievers" interview with Thomas DeLong, HBR.com, https://hbr.org/2011/05/the-hidden-demons-of-high-achi, May 2011.

[10] Sincero, Jen. *You are a Badass: How to Stop Doubting Your Greatness and Start Living an Awesome Life.* Running Press, 2013. p. 39.

**CHAPTER 3**

[11] Jobs, Steve. Prepared text of the Commencement address at Stanford University, June 12, 2005. Stanford.edu. https://news.stanford.edu/2005/06/14/jobs-061505/.

[12] "History of Cognitive Behavior Therapy." Beckinstitute.com. https://beckinstitute.org/about-beck/team/our-history/history-of-cognitive-therapy/, downloaded January 25, 2020.

[13] Beck, J.S. *Cognitive Behavior Therapy: Basics and beyond (2nd ed.).* The Guilford Press, 2011. pp. 19-20

**CHAPTER 4**

[14] Economy, Peter. *"37 Earl Nightingale Quotes That Will Empower You to Soar High."* Inc.com. Accessed January 25, 2020. https://www.inc.com/peter-economy/37-earl-nightingale-quotes-that-will-empower-you-to-soar-high.html.

[15] Clark, Rachel, Michael Freedberg, Eliot Hazeltine and Michelle W. Voss. *"Are There Age-Related Differences in the Ability to Learn Configural Responses?"* Accessed January 25, 2020. https://journals.plos.org/plosone/article?id=10.1371/journal.pone.0137260#abstract0. Published 2015.

[16] *"The Evolution of Dick Tracy's Wristwatch."* Infostory.com. Accessed January 25, 2020. https://infostory.com/2011/01/24/the-evolution-of-dick-tracys-wristwatch/.

[17] *"Video Interview with Marty Cooper."* Sceneworld.org. https://sceneworld.org/blog/2015/02/12/video-interview-with-marty-cooper/. Accessed January 25, 2020.

[18] O'Connell, Jean Gould. *Chester Gould: A Daughter's Biography of the Creator of Dick Tracy.* McFarland. 2007. p. 5.

[19] Peale, Norman Vincent. https://www.goodreads.com/quotes/4324-shoot-for-the-moon-even-if-you-miss-you-ll-land. Accessed February 1, 2020.

## CHAPTER 5

[21] Shapiro, Fred R. *"Who Wrote the Serenity Prayer?"* The Chronicle of Higher Education. https://www.chronicle.com/article/Who-Wrote-the-Serenity-Prayer-/146159/ April 28, 2014. Accessed January 25, 2020.

[22] Housman, Michael and Minor Dylan. *"Toxic Workers."* (PDF) Harvard Business School. Archived from the original (pdf) on 15 August 2019. https://www.hbs.edu/faculty/Publication%20Files/16-057_d45c0b4f-fa19-49de-8f1b-4b12fe054fea.pdf Retrieved 25 August 2019.

[23] *"The High Cost of a Toxic Workplace Culture"* Research Report, SHRM. July 2019. https://www.shrm.org/resourcesandtools/hr-topics/employee-relations/pages/toxic-workplace-culture-report.aspx Accessed January 25, 2020.

## CHAPTER 6

[25] Nin, Anaïs. *Seduction of the Minotaur.* The Swallow Press, 1961. p. 124.

## CHAPTER 7

[26] Thoreau, Henry David. *Walden, and on the duty of civil disobedience.* Thomas Y. Crowell & Company, 1910. p. 357

## ANDREW, PART 2

[27] Tugend, Alina. "Storytelling Your Way to a Better Job or a Stronger Start-Up." New York Times, December 12, 2014.

## CHAPTER 8

[28] Montessori, Maria. Brainyquote.com. https://www.brainyquote.com/quotes/maria_montessori_752858. Accessed February 2, 2020.

[29] *"Why Deepak Chopra Wants You to STOP."* SuperSoul Sunday, Oprah Winfrey Network. YouTube. https://www.youtube.com/watch?v=SFYetaUP7Wg, Jul 1, 2012

[30] Kennedy, John F. Remarks at the Convocation of the United Negro College Fund, Indianapolis, Indiana, April 12, 1959. https://www.jfklibrary.org/archives/other-resources/john-f-kennedy-speeches/indianapolis-in-19590412. Accessed January 25, 2020.

## CHAPTER 9

[32] Tzetzes, John. Book of Histories (Chiliades) 2. Translated by Francis R. Walton. p. 129-130.

[33] "Introducing the Eisenhower Matrix." https://www.eisenhower.me/eisenhower-matrix/. Accessed February 1, 2020.

[34] Covey, Stephen R. The 7 Habits of Highly Effective People: Powerful Lessons in Personal Change. Simon & Schuster, 1989. p. 151.

[35] "How to be More Productive and Eliminate Time Wasting Activities by Using the 'Eisenhower Box'" https://jamesclear.com/eisenhower-box. Accessed February 1, 2020.

[36] Haughey, Duncan. *"A Brief History of SMART Goals."* https://www.projectsmart.co.uk/brief-history-of-smart-goals.php. December 13, 2014. Accessed January 25, 2020.

## CHAPTER 10

[37] Teany, Douglas R. *"Pragmatic Leadership Advice from Donald Rumsfeld."* APPEL Knowledge Services website. https://appel.nasa.gov/2003/01/01/pragmatic-leadership-advice-from-donald-rumsfeld/. January 1, 2003. Accessed January 25, 2020.

[38] Gallo, Amy. *"Why Aren't You Delegating?"* Harvard Business Review. https://hbr.org/2012/07/why-arent-you-delegating. July 26, 2012. Accessed January 25, 2020.

[39] *"You Want it When?"* Institute for Corporate Productivity website. https://www.i4cp.com/news/2007/06/26/you-want-it-when. June 27, 2007. Accessed January 25, 2020.

[40] Henry, Alan. *"Productivity 101: An Introduction to the Pomodoro Technique."* https://lifehacker.com/productivity-101-a-primer-to-the-pomodoro-technique-1598992730. July 12, 2019. Accessed January 25, 2020.

## CHAPTER 11

[42] Friedman, Thomas L. *Thank You for Being Late: An Optimist's Guide to Thriving in the Age of Accelerations* (Version 2.0, With a New Afterword). United States: Picador, 2017. p. 324.

[43] International Coach Federation website. https://coachfedera-tion.org/faqs?fwp_faqs_categories=global-coaching-and-men-toring-alliance-gcma&fwp_faqs_search=definition%20of%20 coaching. Accessed January 25, 2020.

[44] International Coach Federation website. https://coachfederation. org/code-of-ethics. Accessed January 25, 2020.

## CHAPTER 12

[45] Mowat, Dr. Barbara A., Shakespeare, William. *Measure for Measure*. United Kingdom: Simon & Schuster, 2005. p. 35.

[46] Schleckser, Jim. "Nelson Mandela's Secret to Winning." *https://www.inc.com/jim-schleckser/nelson-mandela-s-se-cret-to-winning.html. June 21, 2016. Accessed February 1, 2020.*

[47] Piburn, Sidney D. *Dalai Lama: A Policy of Kindness*. India: Motilal Banarsidass Publishers Pvt. Limited, 2002. p. 40.

[48] Tugaleva, Vironika. *The Art of Talking to Yourself: Self-Awareness Meets the Inner Conversation*. Canada: Soulux Press, 2017.

[49] Williamson, Marianne. *A Return to Love*. United Kingdom: Thorsons, 1996. p. 165.

Terry Boyle McDougall, PCC, MBA, is CEO of Terry B. McDougall Coaching, a Chicago-based consulting firm that specializes in executive coaching, leadership development, talent optimization, and team building. Prior to founding her firm, Terry was a long-time corporate marketing leader. She is a popular keynote speaker and podcast guest. She lives in suburban Chicago with her husband, three children and pet puggle.

For more information, visit www.terrybmcdougall.com

Made in the USA
Monee, IL
04 August 2021

74945306R00213